THE 3-MINUTE MINDSET

THE 3-MINUTE MINDSET

CHOOSE YOUR THOUGHTS. CHANGE YOUR LIFE.

JON ACUFF

BakerBooks
a division of Baker Publishing Group
Grand Rapids, Michigan

Published by Baker Books
a division of Baker Publishing Group
Grand Rapids, Michigan
BakerBooks.com

Printed in the United States of America

Library of Congress Cataloging-in-Publication Data
Names: Acuff, Jon, author
Title: The 3-minute mindset : choose your thoughts. Change your life. / Jon Acuff.
Other titles: Three-minute mindset
Description: Grand Rapids, Michigan : Baker Books, a division of Baker Publishing Group, [2026] | Includes bibliographical references.
Identifiers: LCCN 2026000303 | ISBN 9781540903839 cloth | ISBN 9781493456581 ebook
Subjects: LCSH: Self-actualization (Psychology) | Success
Classification: LCC BF637.S4 A346 2026
LC record available at https://lccn.loc.gov/2026000303

Some names and details have been changed to protect the privacy of the individuals involved.

Published in association with Yates & Yates, www.yates2.com.

Interior design by William Overbeeke

Baker Publishing Group publications use paper produced from sustainable forestry practices and postconsumer waste whenever possible.

26 27 28 29 30 31 32 7 6 5 4 3 2 1

To L.E. and McRae—
hills pay the bills!

CONTENTS

INTRODUCTION

"If you can worry, you can wonder."

That sentence changed my life, but I didn't believe it at first.

I'm cynical by nature. I'm pessimistic at heart. I'm bilingual and my second language is sarcasm. I was therefore very skeptical when I bumped into the concept of mindset in my mid-thirties.

I didn't want to turn a frown upside down. I didn't want to put cheesy posters of cats holding on to ropes and reminding me to "Hang in there!" in my cubicle at work. I didn't want to repeat silly mantras or buy as many candles as I assumed mindfulness required.

But I did want a better job. I did want to write books. I did want to get in shape. I did want to be a great dad and an awesome husband. I did want to learn how to focus and quiet this busy brain of mine. I did want to chase—and, better yet, to catch—all the goals I was capable of. So, despite every apprehension I had, I finally decided to explore the idea of mindset.

I wish I had learned this sooner.

That's what you'll say at the end of this book. You'll probably exclaim, "Why didn't anybody tell me this?" You might even declare, "I should buy multiple copies of Jon's other books, starting with *Soundtracks* and *Procrastination Proof*, to give to everyone I know." (See? I'm sarcastic . . . or maybe not—babies need shoes.) I can't predict that you'll go on a shopping spree when you get to the last page, but I can promise that you will 100 percent wish you had learned how to build your mindset as a teenager.

No one taught us this. There was no mindset class in the eighth grade. They let you graduate from high school without a single lesson on the greatest tool for achievement that's ever been created. Think I'm exaggerating? I'm not.

Every adventure starts with mindset.

Running a marathon? Mindset.

Starting a business? Mindset.

Paying off debt? Mindset.

Building relationships? Mindset.

Repairing them? Mindset.

Mindset is the only skill in the world that offers instant improvement to every part of your life, because it's the only skill you use twenty-four hours a day, seven days a week, 365 days a year. You're always thinking.

Guess what happens when you discover how to really use mindset? You improve every single situation in your life.

But where do you begin? Gratitude? Angry affirmations being yelled at you by a shirtless influencer? Breath work? Cold plunges? An app that gives you a sleep score so you can get an F even while you're unconscious?

Nope.

It's a lot easier than that. You start with a soundtrack.

Soundtracks have been playing in the background of your life since the first day you stormed into the maternity ward. They've been quietly driving every decision, every conversation, and every dream.

Soundtracks are those repetitive thoughts that have just been waiting for you to notice them and build new ones. When I did that in 2008, I was shocked to find out that if you can worry, you can also wonder. Do you know what that means? If you've ever felt stressed, if you've ever been troubled, if you've ever experienced anxiety, you are sitting on a gold mine. Every one of those negative thoughts can be turned into a positive thought. You don't have to become a different person or bury yourself in self-help books. You just have to take the soundtracks you already have and flip them from ones that hold you back into ones that help you.

Put simply, your mindset can be a superpower, not a super problem. Here's how it works:

Great thoughts turn into great actions. Great actions turn into great results.

If you want great results in life, start with great thoughts, or soundtracks, as I like to call them. Then turn those great soundtracks into great actions so that you can easily accomplish great results.

What's the difference between soundtracks and other approaches to mindset?

The goal of meditation is meditation.

The goal of mindfulness is mindfulness.

The goal of gratitude is gratitude.

Those are all noble endeavors, but they won't change your life, write your books, lose your weight, build your business, or accomplish anything tangible and practical.

The goal of soundtracks is results.

Will you have more peace? Certainly. Will you reduce stress? Undoubtedly. Will you have more focus for this noisy world? Of course. But that's just what happens on day one. The real results are always much bigger than that.

Soundtracks are the fastest path to accomplishing any goal you want.

Here's the secret sauce the yoga retreat won't tell you:

Contentment and ambition are not enemies. They're best friends. With the right mindset, you can be both happy and hungry. You can enjoy today and build for tomorrow. It's not an either-or situation. It's both-and.

A friend recently asked me why I work so hard. "Why do you keep writing books, Jon? Why do you keep getting on planes to travel the world and speak to people? Why don't you just enjoy what you already have?"

What a question! I do enjoy what I have. I love my life, but I'm also just getting started. Ask a bird why it still flies. Because it's a bird. That's what it's built to do! Ask a horse why it runs. Because it's designed to gallop! You don't build a new mindset just so you think better. You build a new mindset so you do better, which makes you live better.

Soundtracks and goals go together like peanut butter and jelly. Armed with new soundtracks, you'll be itching to take those winning thoughts for a spin through every goal you've ever had.

That's why I've included two important items with each soundtrack in this book: a question and an action. The question gets you thinking. The action gets you doing.

Don't be surprised if you want to run through the wall like the Kool-Aid Man after reading a soundtrack each morning. Don't be alarmed when every goal feels possible because your playlist is pushing you forward, not pulling you back. Don't be shocked when hard things become easy, anxiety turns into creativity, and personal records get broken.

Are soundtracks really that powerful?

Yes, but don't take my word for it. Experience it for yourself.

Just commit to reading one three-minute soundtrack every day for the next ninety days. As you do, feel free to scribble in the margins. Chances are, my soundtracks will encourage you to write your own. You'll discover broken soundtracks you didn't know were cluttering up your life. And you'll feel validated at how many positive truths you've already been telling yourself internally.

That's why I picked ninety days and not 365. This is a primer, this is the fuse to the dynamite, this is a slingshot that will launch you into a new way of thinking. But guess who is the author of the best soundtracks for your life? *You.*

Once you read this book, you'll have what you need to create a thousand new soundtracks that will take you to a thousand new places.

Ready to go?

Me too.

Welcome to *The 3-Minute Mindset*!

1 You are the cavalry you've been waiting for.

The government won't write your book.

Coworkers won't journal your reasons you should be grateful.

Your boss won't eat your healthy lunch for you.

The next-door neighbor won't burn the midnight oil trying to get your side hustle off the ground.

Even your spouse won't run your miles for you.

You are always the one who has the best shot at changing your life. No one has as much stake in you . . . as you.

You are the cavalry you've been waiting for.

There's an odd moment in adulthood where you realize you are the one who has to pay to repair your air conditioning. In my twenties I remember thinking, "Who's in charge of this roof? Who makes sure the car insurance is current? Who pays this doctor bill?" The answer, much to my initial chagrin, was *me*. Once the shock wore off, I discovered that waiting for someone else to build the life I wanted was a fool's game.

It was a lot more fun to just build it myself. Turns out I was the cavalry I'd been waiting for.

You are the cavalry you've been waiting for. Surround yourself with community for the journey. Friends are an invaluable part of building a remarkable life, but never expect them to do the work that only you can do.

You are the cavalry you've been waiting for.

QUESTION Do you remember the first time you took personal responsibility? What did it feel like?

ACTION Go online and find a photo of a horse and save it to your camera roll. The next time you feel like waiting for the cavalry, look at it and remind yourself, "Giddy up!"

2 Everyone else is making it up too.

I used to think that successful people were probably given a "How to Be an Adult" manual when they were children. At the hospital, when they were born, the doctor said to their parents, "Here's the secret life instructions we give special people. Make sure these don't fall into the wrong hands, specifically Jon Acuff's."

Meanwhile, I was somewhere in my twenties, thirties, and forties and feeling like I was making up the whole thing. I didn't know how to be an adult. I was just riffing and botching so many of the assignments. I kept desperately looking for the manual that would help everything make sense. Then I started meeting successful people. Much to my initial dismay and eventual delight, I discovered that everyone else is making it up too.

I was initially dismayed because I thought there was an instruction book that would instantly answer all of my questions forever. Then I got in greenrooms, boardrooms, and locker rooms and found out no such thing existed. That dismay turned to eventual delight because it meant I could keep making it up too.

At this point, I've met billionaires, ambassadors, professional athletes, and Dolly Parton. (She deserves her own category.) They were all making it up too. They were just doing it with a little more courage and consistency than I was. That's great because courage and consistency are free. I have access to those, and so do you!

If I ever do find someone who has that instruction book, I'll tell you. In the meantime, when you get stressed trying to build a remarkable life, remember: You're not the only one making it up.

We all are.

QUESTION Where in your life do you feel like you're really making it all up as you go?

ACTION Write down three things you "made up" that turned out great.

3 Take the hint, not the hit.

There are three different ways to hear the truth:

1. You tell yourself.
2. Someone else tells you.
3. Life tells you.

Option 1 is the most enjoyable by a long shot. Let's use money as an example.

If you are spending more than you are making and digging a financial hole that will be disastrous later on in life, you can tell yourself that truth. You can take the hint that you're headed toward trouble. You can wake up one day and say, "I've got to make some changes! I'll get a second job, stop going out to eat so much, and put myself on a budget." No sugarcoating for you—just firm, action-inspiring truth.

If you don't tell yourself that, eventually someone else might. A friend will express concern. Your spouse will ask about all the credit card charges. A coworker will comment, "If I were you, I would be stressed with that many bills knocking at my door." This second way is a little embarrassing, but it's still not as bad as the third way.

Life isn't that gentle when it tells you the truth. It tends to hit. You might get your car repossessed. You might get your wages garnished. You might have a financial planner fire you as a client because your situation is so dire. If you ignore yourself and other people, life figures it had better yell to get your attention. The stress-induced heart attack, the job loss because you stopped caring about your career years ago, the spouse who leaves the marriage—when it finally gets to this point, life tends to throw haymakers, not hints.

The good news is you don't have to ever get there. It can all be so much easier. How?

Take the hint, not the hit.

QUESTION On a scale from 1 (never) to 10 (always), how often do you live in denial?

ACTION Practice telling yourself the truth with a small truth today. (Example: If I really want to get to work on time, I have to leave the house fifteen minutes early.)

4 Try again.

Fear is not afraid of your first try. It knows that a lot of people try a lot of things one time. We are a single-serve culture. We're a one-and-done world. We buy exercise equipment we barely use. We purchase home organization systems we hardly open. We get running shoes that stay pristine for a year, forgotten in a closet just as soon as February rolls around.

The first step of any goal is a hobby step. It's dipping a toe in the water.

The second step is everything, especially when the first step didn't go so well.

Why don't most people try again?

1. **The last time really hurt.** Amen. Turns out you're alive. I'd be more worried if you failed and it didn't hurt. That would mean you're numb. I'm sorry it hurt, but I'm glad you noticed. Process it with

a friend or with a counselor if you can afford it. Write about it, shout about it, and then try again.

2. **They want a guarantee.** Me too. I would love a guarantee, but as my friend Al Andrews says, "You get the boat as close to the dock as possible, but at some point, you still have to jump." There's never a guarantee in anything truly good—love, business, health, or money. Try again.
3. **They mentally rehearse the failure.** Stop telling the story about last time, both internally and externally. Every time you do, you're memorizing that regret. The reason you can so quickly access that first attempt is that you've learned it by heart through steady months, if not years, of repetition. It's time to tell some new stories.

Never let your first attempt be your only attempt. Try again.

? QUESTION | What's the last thing you quit too soon? What's the first thing you thought when you read the soundtrack "Try again"?

ACTION | Spend ten minutes trying again on that goal you've been avoiding.

5 Toot your own horn.

I am a professional public speaker. About fifty to sixty times a year, I go to events and deliver keynotes. Often, the company that books me will order a copy of one of my books for all the attendees. Recently, that meant I spent about ninety minutes signing 750 copies of my book *Finish*.

It's what I did after that that I think you should do too. I took a photo of the stack of books and then emailed it to the team who published it. The book has been out for almost ten years. In my message to them, I thanked them for what a wonderful job they did on the book and mentioned how grateful I was that it sold more than 180,000 copies. Why did I do that?

Because you have to toot your own horn.

No one knows what you've been up to. No one has any sense of the hard work you've been putting in. No one is aware of the progress you've been making. It's your job to tell them. You are your own marketing company, even if you never write a book.

Will I ever work with that publisher again? Who knows. But when they think about the name "Jon Acuff," I want them to think, "Isn't he that guy who a decade later is still working hard to sell the book we published?" They didn't know I was in Orlando that night. They didn't know a client bought 750 copies of the book. They didn't know I volunteered to sign every one of them. They do now.

My friend's daughter wants to swim in college. She is being recruited by a few coaches. After her successful showing at a high school championship, her dad encouraged her to email the coaches about her recent accomplishments. She didn't want to and felt like that was bragging. Fortunately, he told her what I just told you: "No one knows what you've been up to." She wrote a short email, and the coaches were all thrilled to hear about her progress.

Do you have to be obnoxious about it? Of course not. Everything you do can be done tactfully. But if you're ever curious about why other people are getting more opportunities at work, getting scholarships at college, and getting to publish books, I'll clue you in on a secret. They're tooting their own horn. You should too.

QUESTION | How much did you cringe reading this one? Be honest.

ACTION | Write and send an email to yourself listing ten amazing things you've done at work this year. Save it and take it to your next annual review.

6 Give gold time to gold tasks.

I don't go to breakfast meetings. I like the foods that come with the meal. Grits are a blast. Scrambled eggs don't miss. I'll even mess around with an early morning burrito. But I don't go to breakfast meetings.

I used to. I was a "let's grab a coffee" guy, but then something simple happened. I realized I'm most creative in the morning. My best thinking time is from 7 to 11 a.m. I'm at my peak during those hours. I can knock out difficult projects, fly through obstacles, and write whole chapters of books with excitement.

Morning time is gold time for me, meaning those are my most valuable hours.

The opposite might be true for you. Maybe the afternoon is when you shine. Maybe late nights are great nights for you. Everyone is different, but the truth is the same for all of us: There's gold in our calendars. Once you find it, you have to protect it.

Meetings are bronze activities for me. I don't need my top creativity to sit through a quarterly update. I don't need my highest energy levels to help a friend find a new job over a latte. I don't need my strongest degree of focus to approve designs for a new project.

When I realized that, I stopped giving gold time to bronze activities.

Want to have a meeting? Great! Let's do it at 4 p.m. on Thursday. Want to pick my brain? Perfect. Let's go for a walk at 5 p.m. on Tuesday. Want my feedback on a budget? Sure. Let's do Wednesday at 3:30 p.m.

Give gold time to gold tasks.

QUESTION | Which hours of the day do you consider gold time? Which tasks do you consider gold tasks?

ACTION | Block out an hour of gold time in your day tomorrow.

7 Success is simple when you make it simple.

I don't work out in the nicest gym in our town. A lot of my friends do and it sounds wonderful. They have more than 100,000 square feet of the latest and greatest machines, a smoothie bar, and you get to ride a pony around in between exercises (probably).

I'm not a member, though, because it's twenty minutes from my house. That's too much friction between me and working out. Friction is any unnecessary difficulty that stands between you and what you want to do.

I can only handle three steps' worth of friction, which is how many it takes me to get to the garage and my home gym. "Gym" is a big word to describe three kettlebells, a set of dumbbells, and a jump rope, but there we are.

If I had to drive twenty minutes every time I went to the gym, I would talk myself out of going most of the time. The friction would pause me just long enough to never work out.

If there's something you're avoiding, make sure you're not falling victim to friction. A sure sign that you are is unnecessary complexity. The simpler you make what you're doing, the more likely you'll do it.

Cleaning your desk on Friday afternoon removes friction from jumping into your week on Monday morning.

Unpacking your suitcase the minute you get back from a trip reduces friction.

Putting your running shoes by the door the night before a morning workout reduces friction.

Polish the process between you and what you want to do until it's so smooth it feels automatic.

QUESTION Imagine you had a magic wand that instantly made life simpler—where would you point it first? Where has something you want to do become too complicated?

ACTION Whichever task you identified, drill it down to one action.

8 Big life, small worries. Small life, big worries.

If you want small worries, live a life so big you don't have time to stress over the little stuff. Do you know where stress grows? In your clock, in your calendar, in the big open chunks of unclaimed time. Rumination needs hours like a fire needs oxygen.

You will never outthink your problems. You can only outact them, and action always fills your schedule, which expands your life. If you're engaged in a life-consuming adventure, you don't have the brain space to replay that dumb thing you said to a coworker last month. You don't have the energy to overanalyze a regret from last year or forecast a disaster that might occur six months from now.

Why do you think your retired uncle is so insufferable about politics? Because he retired too early and now it's all he has. He chose a small life, and now he's got the bandwidth for big worries. He's lost his purpose and has the unused creativity to develop some spicy opinions about a governor of a state he's never even been to!

When I'm writing a new book, I don't have time to get caught up in social media drama. When I'm focused on moving my kids into college, I don't have the space to keep up with the shenanigans of some celebrity. I'm too engaged with a big life to let most things bother me.

When I don't have a mission is when I can camp out on stress for hours at a time. Little things suddenly bother me. Perfectionism points out molehills I turn into mountains because I've got the time to do so.

If you're spending a whole lot of time on a whole lot of things that don't really matter, go find something that does. Sink your teeth into a big project. Find a goal that swallows up your focus. Commit to a race that requires training.

Go all in on your big life and watch your worries shrink.

QUESTION Have you ever felt "lost" in a good way on a big goal or project? What does "all in" look like for you?

ACTION Think of something that's annoying you right now. Decide to let it go and move on.

9 Adults win.

Success is annoyingly simple. Here's the secret: Be an adult. I wish it was more complicated than that because then I could sell you an expensive program, but it's not. All I can sell you are some very affordable actions.

Show up on time. Keep your word. Go above and beyond. Don't gossip. Put others first. Never use the phrase "As my previous email mentioned . . ." Turn in projects when you said you would—or better yet, early. Don't spend more than you make. Don't blow your life up with drugs, alcohol, or affairs. Apologize quickly. Don't be a victim. Spend more time building and less time blaming. Respond to text messages. Write thank-you notes because it forces you to notice all the good things happening in your life. Call your mom once a week. Get enough sleep. Drink water. Eat protein. Learn how to make a few meals at home and then learn how to make a few more. Read books. Go outside as often as you can. Only email or text things you'd be OK with everyone in your company, neighborhood, or family seeing. Avoid ever saying, "That's not my job," "That's not how we do things here," and "I bet that puddle isn't too deep to drive through." It is.

Be an adult because adults win. That's how the world is set up.

How can such ordinary advice give you an extraordinary life? Because no one is doing any of that right now. Not just young generations, although they're often everyone's favorite piñata. People of all ages have forgotten how to be adults. What an opportunity for you! Be an adult and you will stand out as a superstar in every room you enter.

QUESTION Who in your life is adulting exceptionally well? What do you admire most about them?

ACTION Adults write thank-you notes. Write one thank-you note to a friend or coworker.

10 Leave your phone in the other room.

I invented the most advanced technology to help you focus. It eliminates 100 percent of digital distractions, improves every relationship you have, and allows you to sleep more than you ever have before. It's failproof and has been shown to work for anyone of any age who uses it. The best part is that it's 100 percent free and you can start enjoying the benefits today.

What's it called?

Leave your phone in the other room.

I'll admit, the name isn't impressive, but the results are.

When you leave your phone in the other room for even sixty minutes a day, you see instant improvement. For that hour you will not be interrupted by pointless group chats. You will not be tempted to get on Facebook. You won't check the weather in a city you've never been to just because you got curious how things were going there right now. You won't watch five minutes of YouTube that turns into a fifty-minute algorithmic digital buffet. You won't fall prey to a celebrity headline about someone's new nose or old husband.

Instead, you will be able to listen to your spouse or kids in what was once known as a "conversation." You will be able to work a full hour at your job. You will be able to close your eyes at the time you swore you were going to bed. A brief moment of phone-free boredom will quickly be filled with all the things you've been putting off for weeks. How does it work?

Well, later today, tell yourself the soundtrack "Leave the phone in the other room." And then do that. After sixty minutes or so, go retrieve the phone and realize you are suddenly a paragon of self-control. You might be the most disciplined person you know.

I'm giving away this million-dollar idea for free. Not because I'm generous but because I know I'll have even better ideas tomorrow. Why? Because I'm about to leave my phone in the other room.

? QUESTION | Have you ever tried a complicated system to cut down on your screen time? Did it work?

ACTION | Test out this crazy idea for sixty minutes within the next seventy-two hours.

11 Compliments are data, not debates.

"Thank you for the compliment!"

See how easy that was? Say it out loud a few times to get used to it, because if you're anything like me, that soundtrack feels very weird. For most of my life, if you gave me a compliment, I immediately responded with one of the following statements:

"Oh, that? That was nothing."

"That was easier than it looked."

"It could have been better."

When someone gives you a compliment and you immediately reject it, you're not being humble. You're being rude. What you're essentially saying is, "You're wrong. You're dumb if you think that was good. I don't deserve that."

You're throwing a gift back in someone's face. Imagine if you did that at your birthday party. A friend gives you a small present, and without even opening it, you push it back toward them. "No, I don't want this. This isn't for me. I can't accept this."

No one would ever come to your birthday party again.

You might have high standards. You might see legitimate ways you can improve what they're complimenting you about. In the moment you might even feel uncomfortable receiving a little bit of praise. (I do.)

That's OK. It's just data, and now you have a five-word solution you can use for the rest of your life:

"Thank you for the compliment!"

End of story. End of awkwardness. End of denying yourself the kindness of friends. Life comes with enough criticism. Don't make it even harder by campaigning against the positive words too.

Did you enjoy today's soundtrack?

Thank you for the compliment!

QUESTION How easy or difficult is it for you to receive compliments?

ACTION Give one compliment to a friend, coworker, or neighbor. Notice their reaction and how it makes you feel.

12 Go through the motions.

I have some bad news for you: The middle of every goal is boring. It's true. It's natural to lose the sense of excitement and joy that buoyed you at the very beginning. At some point, even a dream feels like drudgery. When this happens, you'll begin to wonder, "Maybe I should quit . . . I'm just going through the motions."

That seems like a legitimate reason to stop.

Who wants to just go through the motions?

I'll tell you who—remarkable people.

Fear will tell you that going through the motions is a problem, a sign you should give up. I will tell you the opposite.

Going through the motions is essential to mastery.

When you master the guitar, you learn the scales.

When you master painting, you repeat the strokes.

When you master any martial art, you duplicate the forms again and again.

If you ever catch yourself going through the motions, congratulations.

It looks like you're becoming a master.

QUESTION What did you do to get reinspired the last time you got bored during the middle of a goal or project?

ACTION Who has mastered a goal you care about (e.g., leader, celebrity, professional athlete, friend)? Write down three things you think they do to get through the boring moments.

13 Learn to walk.

A few times a year, our family road-trips from Nashville, Tennessee, to Boone, North Carolina, to visit my wife's parents. Our favorite place to stop on the journey is the Wendy's on Highway 81 in White Pine, Tennessee. It's the Chick-fil-A of Wendy's, which is the highest compliment you can give in the fast-food industry.

One afternoon, I told the young woman working the drive-through, "This Wendy's is amazing! I bet you have a great manager." She beamed and immediately said, "We do! Her name is Belinda. Let me get her for you." A few seconds later, Belinda came to the window and told me all about her approach to leadership.

"One thing you have to remember about this younger generation is that this is usually their first job. It's not that they have a bad work ethic. They've just never been taught how to work. You have to give them space to learn."

She was right. Think about it: If your one-year-old was struggling with walking, you'd never say, "My baby has a bad walk ethic. What a terrible walker she is." You wouldn't say that because you know it takes time to learn something new.

What if the next time you had to develop a new skill—such as how to use a new software at work, how to raise a teenager versus a tween, or how to care for an aging parent—you gave yourself that same patience?

It's not that you're bad at the new thing. You're just new. You're learning to walk. Again, you'd never tell a six-month-old, "You sure are lazy. It seems like all you do is crawl. Why won't you just walk already?"

Don't say those same things to yourself.

Instead say, "I'm learning to walk."

QUESTION Do you ever expect to be an expert on something you've never done before? What's one new skill you're a toddler at?

ACTION Pick a new hobby, skill, or work project to walk through this week.

14 My head and my heart are friends.

Do you ever feel conflicted? Do you ever feel pulled in more than one direction, especially when you have to choose between different opportunities? Have you ever felt overwhelmed when it comes to picking the best path forward?

Here's why that happens:

Your heart is built for adventure. Your head is built for safety.

Your heart wants to run. It wants to take big risks, chase huge dreams, and go for it, whatever the "it" is. Your head is just the opposite.

Your head wants to think. It wants to weigh all the options. It wants to collect a few more points of data before it makes a decision. It wants to make sure the bridge isn't out before it starts the journey.

You feel conflicted because you are in conflict.

Your heart is built for adventure. Your head is built for safety.

When they work against each other, you feel confused and stuck. When they work with each other, you take calculated risks and make brave, smart decisions.

Negotiate a peace treaty. Give each part of yourself a voice. If you're all heart and no head, you'll live a wildly creative life right up until the moment the bank seizes your house. If you're all head but no heart, you'll have a life full of logic but completely devoid of love.

Make your head and your heart friends.

You'll feel better immediately.

QUESTION Which do you naturally lean on more in life—your head or your heart? What would happen if you switched that for a day?

ACTION Write down one thing your head wants and one thing your heart wants.

15 The growing is in the going.

Sometimes I want to acquire all the skills I need before I attempt the task. I want to be ready for every challenge before I take the first step. I want to make sure I have every resource, tool, and relationship I'll need before I begin.

Unfortunately, that's not how life works.

You don't read a hundred books to learn how to swim. You get in the water.

It's not deep at first. You don't start with open ocean. You don't jump into the North Atlantic on day one, but it's still water. You have to get wet.

You won't ever be "ready" for the most important moments in your life.

You won't be ready for marriage.

You won't be ready for kids.

You won't be ready to write a book.

You won't be ready to start a business.

You won't be ready to move to Colorado and get a master's in wilderness therapy.

You don't grow perfect before the adventure. The adventure shapes you and changes you and challenges you and blesses you every step of the way. The growing is in the going.

One day you look up and find you've been married for thirty years, written a couple of books, kept the weight off, and accomplished all the things you're waiting to start right now.

Don't wait. You'll figure out what you need to know along the way. You'll never know what it really takes to travel the next road until you open the front door and take that first step.

? QUESTION | What's one area of your life where you've been waiting to feel "ready"?

ACTION | Take the first step for the first goal that came to mind while reading this entry.

16 Today is sacred.

It might look like an average Tuesday, but it's not.

There's no such thing as an average day when we're guaranteed none and given this one.

Today is sacred. It's an invitation to where the fields meet the forest. This is edge country, where anything is possible and everything is promised. Today is always uncharted territory because today has never happened before. This is today's first and last performance. Today is much like you: one of one.

Sometimes I want a guarantee. Before the day begins I want to know that everything will go my way. I procrastinate until the coast is clear. I want an assurance that today will hold no challenges or inconveniences. I do not want to be stretched, I want to be served, but the day is too wild for that. The day speaks in dares, not formulas.

Fair enough, I think, on many a morning. If the day won't meet my expectations, perhaps the safest bet is to have none. Your hopes can't be dashed if you pre-dash them yourself and pretend they do not exist. We accept the automatic F of never trying because we fear the C-minus of giving it our all and falling short.

That's a popular approach, but killing your dreams because you're afraid they might get bruised is a trade-off you should never make.

I refuse to accept that any longer.

I don't. I won't.

I choose mystery. I choose wonder. My fear has not dissipated. My thoughts launch couch campaigns and beg me to stay at home. Procrastination swims so close to the surface I can see its every scale.

My feelings are not fully on board. They may never be, but I can no longer wait for unanimous agreement. The vote is split, my heart and head divided, but I have veto power in my right foot. It's already out the door, and that's all it takes.

Life won't wait and neither will we.

QUESTION When is the last time you did something completely unexpected, something outside of your normal character? How did you feel afterward?

ACTION Schedule an "adventure" day where you plan a few hours to try something new.

17 Perfectionism is just fear wearing a tuxedo.

Perfectionism likes to masquerade as a character trait, doesn't it? It's a rascal like that. In job interviews, when asked about our weaknesses, we hem and haw and finally confess, "I struggle with perfectionism. I guess my main issue is that I have such a high standard of quality."

Stop it.

Perfectionism is a poison that pretends to be a vitamin. It is not an asset that helps you improve your work but a danger that prevents you from ever finishing your work.

There is always one more edit you need. There is always one more bit of data you must gather. There is always one more *i* you must dot and *t* you must cross. Then it will be perfect.

This is the promise, but perfectionism never completes anything. It can't, because nothing is ever good enough. Perfectionism doesn't even know how to say the phrase "We're done," because you never are. It doesn't set a standard of high quality. On the contrary, it creates a mythical finish line you will never reach.

Be excellent.

Be demanding even.

Reach for the stars, just don't expect perfectionism to get you there. If you give it the moon, it will suggest that the Milky Way might be even better.

? QUESTION How do you feel when you read the phrase "good enough"? Does that feel like failure or like a level of completion that allows you to actually finish projects?

ACTION Take a small goal to 90 percent and then declare it done. See if anyone even notices the missing 10 percent. (Spoiler alert—they won't.)

18 Hills pay the bills!

Today, I will arrive in Miami at midnight.

That wasn't the initial plan. My original flight was supposed to arrive at 4 p.m., but original flights have a funny way of getting canceled in Nashville in the spring.

A few weeks ago, after traveling all night to reach Atlanta, I finally arrived at 4 a.m. for a 7 a.m. meeting with a client. I don't know if you're bad at math, but that's not awesome.

One time, when the Wichita airport was a no go, I got rerouted to Manhattan, Kansas. You know, the Little Apple. I got into a tiny rental car and then drove through the night, dodging deer and disappointment the entire way. I had a speech to give to a credit union in the morning.

Do you know what I said to myself a hundred times in each of those moments and the many more challenges I've experienced in fifty years on this planet?

Hills pay the bills!

If I do the work that others don't, I get to experience vistas others won't. The obstacles aren't against me, they're for me, because they're making it that much harder for other people to keep up. Everybody can do it when it's easy. The hills are where you make the real difference, because only those who are all in keep going.

I hope your next flight is on time.

I hope your next boss is the best.

I hope every client pays all their invoices on time at your company.

But the next time anything remotely negative happens to you, I hope you'll see it as an opportunity to shine, not shrink.

Hills pay the bills!

QUESTION When you run into an obstacle, what's the first soundtrack you usually think? Does it help you or hurt you?

ACTION Get a tattoo that says "Hills pay the bills!" Or write it on a sticky note. Your choice, really.

19 My time is valuable *and* vulnerable.

I unsubscribed from Netflix a few years ago, and here's the crazy thing: I did not die. It's true. I'm still alive.

Now granted, when friends ask me if I've seen the latest season of *Love Bachelor Shark Dance Mom Island*, I have to say no. But other than that, it's been pretty good.

Why did Jenny and I decide to kick Netflix to the curb? We've had it since it was delivered in the mail. If you're young, I just blew your mind. The United States Postal Service used to bring you Netflix, and queue management was everything! We're fans of the service, but after fifteen years of subscribing, we realized something:

Time is the most valuable resource we have, but it's also the most vulnerable.

Time can't protect itself. Only we can protect it. Sometimes that means canceling services like Netflix. Their goal is to get as much of my time as possible. My goal is to keep as much of it as possible. We are at odds, my friend.

Same goes with Instagram, X, Facebook, YouTube, Disney+, Paramount+, Peacock, Hulu, and Amazon Prime. You are their business model. They have a little chart in an office somewhere that says, "Turn Laura's attention into revenue" (or Tim's, or whatever your name is). They are coming for your time, and every year they get better at stealing it without you even noticing.

I see how it is. Game on, streaming services. Heads up, though—this is my twelfth book. I already know what it's going to cost me to write the next one: *time.*

There's not a single episode of *Love Bachelor Shark Dance Mom Island* that will be more exciting than holding that finished book in my hands.

My time is valuable *and* vulnerable.

QUESTION | What is your biggest time waster?

ACTION | Open Screen Time, find the app you used the most last week, and then come up with a plan to use it 25 percent less this week.

20 I make my own hindsight.

"Hindsight is 20/20."

That's what they say, right? If you had known how bad the traffic was on the highway, you would have taken back roads. If you had known that business deal wouldn't work, you would have passed on it a year ago. If you had known the later flight would get canceled, you would have taken the earlier one.

Or maybe you've heard "Experience is the best teacher," which is just another version of that classic soundtrack. Once you've had the experience and reflect on it with hindsight, it's easy to see what the best path forward was.

This is true, but where does it say you have to wait for hindsight?

What if you could make your own hindsight?

If I want to know whether an idea is going to work in a book, I don't wait until after the book is published to find out. I first post it on Instagram and read the reactions in the comments. Now I've got a little hindsight that didn't cost me much. Then I expand the idea and put it in a newsletter. More hindsight. Then I turn it into a podcast episode. Additional hindsight. Then I teach it in an online course. Hindsight. Then I add it to a speech and share it with a live audience. Hindsight.

By the time I write the idea in a book, I've got 20/20 vision about it. Not because I'm a fortune teller but because I created fast experiences that gave me hindsight.

Will you love the exercise classes at that new gym? Take three of them and find out before you sign a long contract. Make your own hindsight.

Will that employee work out at your company? Give them a one-month, paid project to test their abilities before you hire them full-time. Make your own hindsight.

Will you enjoy gardening as much as you think you will? Grow basil in a pot before you completely dig up your backyard with grandiose plans because you got inspired by someone on Instagram. Make your own hindsight.

The faster you act on your goals in small ways, the faster you'll get experience, and the deeper your hindsight will grow.

QUESTION What impulsive purchase or grand action have you made because you were impatient? What smaller action would have given you a better chance for hindsight?

ACTION Find a small seven-day, one-day, or one-hour audition you can do before you commit to your next idea.

21 Never expect rational decisions from irrational people.

"Can you believe that bank robber asked for a helicopter?"

I can, because his first decision was to rob a bank.

File this soundtrack under "How to save yourself copious amounts of stress with the people you love."

The friend who quit their job without another job, the one who is hoping the universe will take care of his bills and skipped out on the interview you set up for him, is being irrational right now. You could get mad at him for not being more responsible and attending the interview, but nothing he does is going to be rational right now.

You could continue to give him advice he won't take, show him the dangers of his risky decisions, which he thinks were great, and struggle to drag him out of a hole he seems content in, but even writing that sentence was exhausting. Imagine living it.

Here's a bonus soundtrack that isn't fun to admit but will free you up from lots of unnecessary stress:

It's hard watching people you love make life harder than it needs to be.

It happens sometimes. To all of us. This is a soundtrack/apology to my parents who couldn't make me see straight in high school.

The only person you can force to change is you. The faster you come to grips with that, the more you can forgive yourself and that irrational person too. You might even find ways to enjoy them a little bit once you've freed yourself from trying to convince them to make better decisions they don't want to make yet.

QUESTION | Who was the person that immediately came to mind when you read this soundtrack?

ACTION | Call that person.

22 My work is not my identity.

Sometimes criticism crushes me. A one-star review wrecks my day. An online barb served up via Instagram knocks me off course. A comment via email throws me for a loop.

Why do I get stuck so easily by random strangers and their words? Because I've confused my work with my identity. That is a mistake.

Your work is not your identity. It's not who you are, it's a by-product of knowing who you are. The difference is subtle but critical. If you believe that what you do is who you are, when people criticize it, you receive the criticism very differently. They are not commenting on your business or job, they are commenting on your soul. Your very identity is up for grabs for the faceless internet masses if you make the mistake of thinking you are your work.

You are not.

I am not.

I write books. This is my latest one.

That is my work.

When someone criticizes my books, they have not criticized me. They have commented on something I created, not who I am. The challenge is that to create your best work, you have to put your identity into it. You must lean into it with your heart, pouring into the project with the very best of who you are. But once it is created, once it is finished, you have to divorce yourself from it in a way. You gave it your heart, but you did not leave your heart with the project.

You took your heart with you so that you can create something else with it next time.

You are bigger than a job or a song or a project or an anything.

Your identity is not up for grabs.

Your work is.

And those are two very different things.

QUESTION | Have you ever overreacted to criticism about your work?

ACTION | Tell the world about something you're working on. For example, post it online, send an email, or share it with a friend. If you receive negative feedback, say thank you and let it go.

23 The sooner I start, the sooner I finish.

It takes me about one thousand hours to write a book.

If I average fifteen hours of writing a week, that's a sixteen-month project. Oof. That is discouraging.

A mountain that big doesn't motivate me—it freezes me. That's a lot of work. Imagine if your boss told you tomorrow, "Here's your new task. I'd like you to spend the next year and a half chipping away at this thing."

I'm too unfocused, too undisciplined, and too unorganized to write a whole book. And yet . . . I keep figuring out a way to do it. One soundtrack that makes the whole thing a lot more manageable is "The sooner I start, the sooner I finish."

I want to be finished right now. That's always what the impatient side of me demands. *Let's finish right this second. Let's get this thing done!* Recognizing that desire and realizing I can't "binge finish" a project that big, I remind myself that the person who controls the clock is me. If I start today, the clock starts ticking. Even that first hour, though it feels insignificant, is a step in the right direction. If I do that ten days in a row, I'll be ten hours closer to that finish line.

It might only be 1 percent progress, but 99 percent of people won't make it there. I'm already ahead of the game.

If you have a goal that feels massive, start today. The sooner you do, the sooner you're done.

QUESTION What's the biggest project you ever completed? How long did it take?

ACTION Identify a 1 percent action that will lead to 1 percent progress and schedule it within the next seven days.

24 Only take advice from people you'd hire at your own company.

Business philosopher Jim Rohn is credited with the soundtrack "You are the average of the five people you spend the most time with." He's right. You become the company you keep. Show me your friends and I will show you your future.

But how do you decide who to spend time with? There are a million qualities, characteristics, and personality traits that make up a person, so how do you determine who gets to shape you?

Let's add a soundtrack to Jim's to make the whole process a lot easier.

Only take advice from people you'd hire at your own company.

I don't mean the company you work for. I mean you should imagine starting your own small business. Every dollar counts. Every hire is critical. Would you hire all five of your closest friends right now? If you had to hitch your wagon to their stars, would you?

I bet a few of your friends are an instant "Yes!" You'd love to build a company alongside them, fighting your way together from the garage start-up moments to the big leagues.

I bet a few of them are a no. They've got a temper that pops off too casually. They're prone to gossip. They invented quiet quitting and hardly give any effort at their current job. Guess what you will be tempted to do if you keep allowing them to impact your life? All of those negative qualities too.

Filtering your friendships is a weird thing to think about, but the impact they're having on who you are today and who you will be tomorrow is massive.

Choose your friends carefully.

QUESTION

Has a close friend ever given you bad advice? What was the outcome?

ACTION

Write down the names of people you would hire. If someone gives you advice, now you have a list to refer to. If they're not on it, you can be like a bouncer at an exclusive club: "I'm sorry, I don't have your name on my list."

25 Mo' money, less problems.

Most of the soundtracks in this book are fresh-out-of-the-box, brand-new ideas. Some of them, though, are direct counterattacks to popular broken soundtracks. Guess which one this is?

"Mo' money, mo' problems" is a soundtrack people say to describe what happens if you become successful. If you make more money, the stress in your life will increase. A bigger bank account comes with bigger issues. Extra success comes with extra stress.

Hogwash.

That's not even a little true.

Have you ever had "no money"? I have, and it didn't come with "no problems." It actually made every problem I had so much worse. If your car's transmission goes out when you don't have money, that is a major, life-altering problem. If your transmission goes out when you have some money, that is a minor inconvenience.

The reason this broken soundtrack made the list is that I've watched it trick too many people into pulling back from success. One of the main reasons people self-sabotage is that they think a bigger life will come with bigger trouble. They're afraid they can't handle that and then drill holes in their own boat to make sure they sink it before it leaves the harbor. Don't do that.

At the same time, let's keep it honest. I said "less problems," not "no problems," because even if you're a billionaire you might need a root canal, have a car crash, or get bit by a Komodo dragon. If that last one feels very specific, it's because that's what happened to Sharon Stone's husband when she gave him a backstage private tour at the LA Zoo. That guy was very rich, but as everyone knows, Komodo dragons don't respect wealth.

At least he could afford to pay for the reconstructive foot surgery. True story.

Mo' money, less problems.

? QUESTION Do you have any broken soundtracks when it comes to money? What are they?

ACTION Write down three things that make life easier that you're grateful you can afford.

26 The road to awesome is always paved with awkward.

I have an awesome life. I want you to have one too. That's why I write books like this. Life is far too long to settle for average. That said, I must warn you: Awesome lives come with a lot of awkwardness. Average lives come with a lot less.

How can that possibly be?

Well, in an average life you get to stay deeply ensconced in your comfort zone. You don't ever have to stretch. You don't have to learn new things. You're never challenged. You don't have to change. You can photocopy each day of your life, never deviating an inch from the repetitiveness of a vanilla existence.

Did that last paragraph feel a little boring? I hope so. You were built for adventures, not errands. You were built for awesome. When you realize that, you will be required to do some awkward things. I didn't know that when I got started.

My first book signing was awkward. My first speech was awkward. My first blog was awkward. My first half marathon was awkward. My first time trying CrossFit was awkward. It's hard for me to think of a single example where something new wasn't awkward.

Initially, I felt like maybe it was me, but along the way I learned something very freeing: The road to awesome is always paved with awkward. Awkwardness isn't failure, it's a sign I'm being brave. (It might be the only way to become brave, because I usually don't need courage until I feel awkward.)

Awesome and awkward are not enemies. If anything, they've got a symbiotic relationship, like those small birds that hop around on the backs of crocodiles. They work together.

The next time you feel awkward, congratulate yourself. You must be doing something new, and you're probably on the verge of something awesome.

? QUESTION | When was the last time you learned something new? Did it feel awkward?

ACTION | Find your friend who is never afraid to do something new and ask them what their secret is.

27 I'm not most people.

Most people who want to write a book never do. In fact, according to *The New York Times*, 82 percent of Americans want to write a book. Less than 1 percent of those actually do.[1]

Most people put the weight back on after a diet. In fact, 95 percent of people regain the weight they lost within a year.

Most people quit their New Year's resolutions in January. In fact, according to the University of Scranton, 92 percent of all New Year's resolutions fail.[2]

Most people mortgage their dreams to TV. In fact, according to Nielsen data reports, the average American watches TV thirty-two hours a week.[3]

Here's the good news though: We're not most people.

You and I don't have to open that invitation to be ordinary. We don't have to join the crowd. We don't have to settle.

Most people don't read books like this, but you are. Guess what that means? You're not most people.

Do you know why it's so fun to get up early and jog, write, or scale a business before the rest of the world is awake? Because in that moment you're not most people. Few things in the world are as satisfying as that feeling, and it's available for free every day. But most people won't do the extra rep. Most people won't call the extra client. Most people won't go the extra mile.

That's OK.

We're not most people.

QUESTION What's one small way you can stand out from the crowd this week?

ACTION Set your alarm for fifteen minutes earlier tomorrow and see if I'm telling the truth.

28 I'm just getting started!

Chisel this one on my tombstone.

My poor team is tired of hearing me say, "We're just getting started," but it's true. I don't care whether you're ten years into a career or thirty years into a marriage, this soundtrack will give you fresh eyes for the road ahead.

I started saying this one when my business turned ten. I was proud of how far we'd come, but I was also thrilled with how much runway there was left. Culture preaches the opposite. If you're not careful, they'll convince you it's too late.

It's too late to start your business.

It's too late to run a marathon.

It's too late to get married.

It's too late to become a homeowner.

Nope, those are broken soundtracks. If you're breathing, it's not too late, especially if you transform this new soundtrack into action. The fun thing is that it works in every area of your life, including parenting.

I mistakenly thought that once my kids turned eighteen, I was kind of done with parenting. I might not have said that out loud, but I thought parenting adult children would be easier than raising young kids. Whoops. My bad. Turns out, parenting adult children is even more challenging. My friend David Ashcraft explained it perfectly: "The stakes are higher. When your eighth grader doesn't make the volleyball team, that's sad. When your twenty-eight-year-old gets a divorce, that's tragic."

Noted.

I'm not done building my business.

I'm not done getting in shape.

I'm not done parenting.

Turns out, I'm just getting started!

QUESTION | Have you ever felt like it's "too late" to start something new?

ACTION | Start that.

29 Friends hire friends.

"Nepo baby" is a popular term to describe celebrities' kids who are given breaks the rest of us didn't get. I for one would have loved to be the son of Keanu Reeves and given a leading role in *John Wick 27*. Dare to dream. Is nepotism really a big problem though? Most of the time people who complain about nepotism are just failing to understand a soundtrack that has existed since Neanderthals lived in caves:

Friends hire friends.

People hire people they know and like. Life is rarely a meritocracy. Maybe it would be fairer if it was, but it's not. Bemoaning this fact is a tremendous waste of time.

A much simpler truth is that people give opportunities to people they enjoy. Go figure. They give a hand up to someone who was nice to them at a previous company.

They open a door for their kid because . . . she's their kid. Knowing that, what should you do in your own life?

1. **Burn fewer bridges.** Every industry is smaller than you think. You're going to see those people you don't like again at another job in the future. Make as few enemies as you can.
2. **Be friendly.** There will never be a day where you say, "I wish I had fewer friends." This is bigger than just career, of course. A friend will tell you, "I know a house you'd love to buy" before it's officially listed. A friend will tell you which vendor has the best tomatoes at the farmers' market before they sell out. A friend will save you a seat at a movie because you're running late. Was that nepotism? No, they just wanted to sit next to their friend.
3. **Give without keeping score.** Help others without the expectation that they will help you in the exact same way. That's how you build friendships, not just transactions.

If you do those three things, you'll never be out of work for very long. Why? Because friends hire friends.

Make as many as you can. And Keanu, if you're reading this right now, "Jon Reeves" has a nice ring to it. Adoption might still be an option.

QUESTION | Who is the last friend that did something kind for you?

ACTION | Write that friend a thank-you note.

30 The faster I ask for help, the faster I'll get it.

If you lose your job, make a list of all the friends who can help you find a new one. Then write a short email or text message and let them know you're looking for work.

Don't wait another minute. An hour after you've been laid off or fired, start your list. Why?

The faster you ask for help, the faster you'll get it.

This soundtrack goes against everything you'll want to do. When we experience challenges, it's human nature to hide. It's embarrassing to lose your job. It's frightening to go through a financial crisis. It's scary to have health issues. We tend to isolate in moments like that, when what we should be doing is asking for help. Quickly. Constantly. Consistently.

People can't help you unless they know you need help. If you wait a week or a month, do you know what your friend is going to say when you finally reach out? "I wish you had told me sooner."

Is this one easy to live out? Nope. It costs a bit of vulnerability, but it's worth it. Whatever you're going through right now, you're not meant to go through it alone.

Ask for help.

The faster you do, the faster you'll get it.

? QUESTION What's the hardest part of asking for help? When was the last time you did?

ACTION Find someone in your life who needs help today, tomorrow, or this week. Help them.

31 Finish the day, not the work.

Have you ever gone to bed a bit frustrated and thought to yourself, "I didn't get everything done today"? Have you ever left your office and felt discouraged because despite all your best efforts, you barely made a dent in your to-do list? Have you ever worked hard to clean your house and still felt like you didn't get everything accomplished?

Do you know why that happens?

You tried to finish the wrong thing.

Work is not designed to be finished. It is built bottomless. If you're a teacher, you will never go home at night and say, "I helped every student the exact perfect amount today." If you are a vice president at a company, you will never say, "I completely solved every problem our industry has." If you are doing housework, you will never say, "I have finally done all the laundry forever."

Hopefully you laughed at that last example because you know it's impossible. Even as you do the laundry today, you are wearing clothes that will become tomorrow's laundry. You can be angry about that or accept a simple principle:

You don't finish work, you finish the day.

When you do, it's easier to stop beating yourself up. You'll give yourself a little grace for the items on your list that didn't get done. You'll admit that your empty inbox will be full again tomorrow. The to-do list will grow a little overnight. The housework will multiply like rabbits while you sleep. Who keeps taking off their socks in the kitchen?

Make peace with that and, better yet, celebrate that you did finish the day. Monday is in the books. Wednesday has been vanquished. Friday has been completed. Days come to a perfect close every time your head hits the pillow. Celebrate that instead of overfocusing on the fact that you did not get everything done.

Finish the day, not the work.

QUESTION What's the most frustrating thing you can't seem to finish? How could you see the endless nature of it as a good thing, not a bad thing?

ACTION Grab a sticky note. Write "I finished the day" on it and put it on your bedside table as your reminder tonight.

32 Never give the problem a year and the solution a week.

"This exercise plan isn't working."

Friends tell me that occasionally.

The new diet, new workout, new anything is not working and they are discouraged. In that situation I always ask two questions. The first is, "How long have you been doing it?"

The answer is usually, "About three weeks."

The second question I ask is, "How long did it take you to gain the weight you are trying to lose?"

The answer is usually, "About three years."

Right there's the issue with most goals. We give the problem three years to develop and the solution three weeks to work. When it doesn't, we get frustrated and think something must be wrong.

Never give the problem a year and the solution a week.

If it took you five years to get into financial debt, it might take more than five weeks to get out. If it took you three years to fill your attic with junk, it might take you more than three days to deal with it. If a relationship with a family member deteriorated over a decade, it might take more than one Thanksgiving to repair it. Be generous with the amount of time you give yourself when you're working on a goal. This simple approach applies to more than just problems too.

If you've been using the same software at work for ten years, it might take you longer than ten days to learn the new one. If it took you three years to feel connected in your last neighborhood, it might take longer than three months to feel connected in the new one.

I want instant results in my life. Who doesn't? But the best things always take longer than I want. The next time progress feels slow, double or even triple the amount of time you're giving it. You remove the pressure and enjoy the process a lot more that way.

? QUESTION | What is one area of your life where you might be expecting faster results than is reasonable?

ACTION | Double the time you're giving yourself for results on a small goal. For instance, if you want to write 1,000 words for your book this week, give yourself two weeks to do it instead.

33 You can't spell "extraordinary" without "weird."

Wait, that's not right, is it? At least the bumper sticker that says "Earth without art is just 'eh'" makes sense. The word "art" is clearly in the middle of the word "earth." Fair enough, but the soundtrack stands. If you want to be extraordinary, you will be weird.

You have to be, because otherwise you'd be ordinary. The very definition of "extraordinary" guarantees that you are not normal. This creates a tension. On the one hand you want to stand out, you want to leave a mark in the world, you want to impact people in a special way. Great! Me too. On the other hand, you want to fit in. You don't want to get criticized or laughed at. Me too. What do we do?

Learn to accept the five stages of innovation:

1. **Weird.** It always starts here. The thing you create is so outside the norm that you get made fun of.
2. **Unusual.** You stick to it long enough that people start to notice it's different in a good way.
3. **Unique.** Now the special side of it shows through and it gets complimented. "Look at this fresh approach to life you discovered."
4. **Obvious.** This just makes sense. Why haven't we always done it this way?
5. **Common.** It's so ordinary that you can't even remember a time when it didn't exist.

Every product you couldn't dream of living without went through those five stages. I'm talking about Uber, Netflix, and the iPhone. Even the entire internet seemed too weird to work when it debuted.

In 1998, Paul Krugman famously said, "By 2005 or so, it will become clear that the Internet's impact on the economy has been no greater than the fax machine's."[4] Whoops.

Who is Paul Krugman, you ask? A Nobel Prize–winning economist! The internet was too weird for him. He was spectacularly wrong. Someone should have told him this soundtrack:

"You can't spell *extraordinary* without *weird*."

Be weird. It's the only way to really stand out, and if your goal was to fit in, you wouldn't be reading this book.

? **QUESTION** | Has anyone ever called one of your ideas weird? How did you respond?

ACTION | Tell a friend you trust about a new idea that excites you.

34 I trust friends who love me enough to tell me things I might not like to hear.

File this one under "Easy to say, hard to do, but worth it."

Do you know why famous, successful people surround themselves with yes-men? Because it's easier to believe you're amazing when everyone is telling you that you're amazing. Do you know what happens to those people though? Turn on TMZ.

The truth is that 100 percent self-awareness is impossible. We can't completely see ourselves. We always need friends who encourage us, inspire us, and occasionally give us feedback. Those first two are fun, but that last one is foundational. Feedback from a friend allows you to get better. It enables you to tweak behavior, improve habits, and grow every part of your life.

More than a decade ago, a friend told me that my speeches felt "rehearsed and robotic." He said that because (1) they were and (2) he cared about me. I was new to public speaking and was over-rehearsing. I had the speeches so memorized that they felt wooden. I couldn't see that though. It took a few words from a friend to break the spell and help me get better.

Would I have rather he just told me, "Jon, you are already the best"? Sure, my ego would have preferred that, but his truthful comment gave me the spark to raise my game in wonderful ways.

Foster friendships where each person is committed to helping the other person become their best version. Make sure the people in your corner have the freedom to tell you the truth.

? QUESTION | Have you ever overreacted when someone gave you critical feedback?

ACTION | Find someone you trust (e.g., spouse, coworker, leader, friend) and ask them for feedback. When they share it, just say "thank you" and then spend a little time thinking about how you can incorporate it into your life.

35 Eat fewer Oreos.

Boooo! What kind of nonsense soundtrack is "Eat fewer Oreos"? Jon Acuff, you monster!

Hold up. Hear me out before you cookie-cancel me.

One week, I noticed on my Screen Time app that I had spent thirteen hours on Instagram. That was a bit of a shock, because if you'd asked me how much time I'd used it, I would not have guessed nearly two hours a day. That felt like an awful lot, and to be honest, I never feel particularly great after a long doomscrolling session. I'm certainly not energized. I think the scientific name for the feeling I have is "bleh."

But it's hard to put that much screen time into context, so I decided to reframe into something that was easier to understand: Oreos. (This is how my brain works.) If every five minutes I gave to pointless digital consumption on Instagram was like eating an Oreo, how many Oreos would that make in a week? The answer was 156 Oreos, or twenty-two a day.

If I told you that every day I eat twenty-two Oreos, would you love me enough to have an intervention? Would you hide my milk? Would you check my bank statements for bulk purchases from Nabisco? I hope so, because clearly I have a problem.

Could I act surprised at feeling sluggish or unmotivated if I was eating nearly two dozen Oreos a day? Not really. So then why am I surprised I'm having a hard time being present in conversations, finding time to exercise, or struggling to write if I'm using Instagram two hours a day?

If you looked at hours as Oreos, you might find it a lot easier to create a few boundaries for your day. Feel free to dunk one or two—who doesn't love an Oreo? But if you're spending four times the amount of time online that you are exercising, don't be shocked when you come down with a serious case of bleh.

QUESTION What's your favorite way to waste time online? How much time did you spend doing that last week?

ACTION Set a thirty-minute daily maximum for your favorite app, and see if you can stick to it for three days.

36 Advice is à la carte.

I became a morning person in my mid-thirties. Prior to that, I was a "wake up at sevenish" (emphasis on the *ish*) type of guy. I might even sleep in until nine o'clock on a Saturday. I hated getting up early. Kids and a desire to write myself out of a job I didn't enjoy changed that though. Early morning was the only time I could write my blog, so early bird, here I came.

Now I'm one of those annoying people who gets up at 5 a.m. with a smile. By 7 a.m. I've read my Bible, had coffee, journaled, and worked out. Twenty-one-year-old me would be aghast at fifty-year-old me. I'm a morning person now, but maybe you're not.

The problem with books like this is that they are often written as if what worked for me will work exactly the same way for you. Have you ever read a personal development book and felt discouraged instead of encouraged? That's because you didn't know this soundtrack yet.

Advice is à la carte.

When you read a self-help book, listen to a podcast, or have a coffee with a wise friend, you're not supposed to take all the advice. There's no one-size-fits-all when it comes to wisdom. You're supposed to listen intently and then pick out the handful of things that fit your personality, strengths, and unique circumstances. Otherwise you'll feel like a failure when you try to do everything someone else suggested and it doesn't work for you.

My wife and I are empty nesters. We prefer to say we're on a road show, because "empty nest" sounds like you're a thousand years old. On the weekends we have to look for activities to fill our time. If I wanted to write, exercise, or pursue a hobby for three hours on Saturday, I could. Know what I couldn't do when we had toddlers? Any of that.

Imagine if I said, "In order to have peace in your life, practice 'Slow Saturdays.' Give yourself the first three hours of the day to enjoy whatever you like doing most." You couldn't tell your toddlers, "I read a book that said I need me time, so if you guys could not put forks directly into every electrical outlet in the house for the next three hours, that would be great."

Your circumstances are different, so you wouldn't follow that advice exactly. That's always how wisdom goes. Pick and choose what works best for you. Follow the tips that do. Ignore the ones that don't. If you're a night owl, never let us morning people shame you.

Advice is à la carte.

? QUESTION | Have you ever tried a system someone suggested that didn't work for you? How did you feel about it?

ACTION | For any soundtrack that works so well for you that you test out the action, put a star beside it in the table of contents so it's easy to remember.

37 I get it in where I can fit it in.

Life would be a lot easier if you could get into a routine.

It would be amazing if every day were the same and you could fit in a goal—exercising, for example—like a piece in a puzzle that never changes week to week. Unfortunately, that's not how life works.

No two weeks are the same for me.

No two months are the same for me.

No two years are the same for me.

I fight for routine, I really do, but life is just messier than all the perfect plans I make.

If the success of my goals depended on me always having the same routine, I'd be screwed.

I travel for work. I have kids. I have projects that come up out of nowhere. I have commitments that take longer than I expected. I get flat tires. The crawl space floods. A cough passes through every member of our house.

When that happens, I tell myself a simple rhyme: "I get it in where I can fit it in."

If I wait for a perfect week without distractions and complications before I exercise, I will never move a muscle. That's why I run at odd hours in odd hotels on odd treadmills. Would I have preferred to jog around my neighborhood early in the morning like I sometimes get to? Sure, but guess what? I have work in LA, Dallas, and Costa Mesa, so I have to exercise in the most depressing "fitness centers" instead. Can we all just admit that one treadmill and seven dumbbells in a windowless room next to the ice maker does not a fitness center make?

Most weeks aren't shaped perfectly to my needs. I have to squeeze in exercise, writing, and meetings where I can. I have to get it in where I can fit it in.

Stop waiting for a perfect week where your family will give you hours to do meal prep, research your side hustle, or clean the garage from top to bottom. Stop waiting for a perfect week where you have gobs of time. Stop waiting for a perfect week that is wide open for all your needs.

It's not coming. Start with the messy week you've got and get it in where you can fit it in.

QUESTION | What's the activity or goal you most often put off until you have "more time"?

ACTION | Fit in fifteen minutes on that activity today.

38 Bring staples to knife fights.

Do you have a job? Me too! There are a handful of situations everyone reading this book will experience, and one of them is definitely work. You might not write a book, run a half marathon, or start a business, but chances are that you have a career.

Want a simple way to make it phenomenal? Bring staples to knife fights.

The next time you have a meeting, come prepared. Do a little research. Ask a few questions of the key participants beforehand. Gather some information. Then put it into a document thick enough that it requires a staple. When everyone else in the room rambles on, as the unprepared always do, quietly wait for the right moment and then say, "I spent some time working on this challenge and have a few thoughts."

When you hand them out, people are going to look at you like you're the mayor of Go-Getter Town. "Whoa, when did you do this?" they will ask. "That's a really good point," they will say, since you are more than likely the only one who took the time to write down their point ahead of time. "Thanks for coming so prepared to talk through this," clients will exclaim.

To be clear, you didn't spend a hundred hours on this task—you probably spent only two. But in a world where fewer and fewer people show up to meetings prepared, you are going to automatically look like a superstar. A single staple might weigh less than a tenth of an ounce, but the impact could change your entire career.

Most meetings are knife fights to some degree. Co-workers are jockeying to be heard and respected. Go the extra mile and show up with a staple.

? QUESTION How would you personally define "well-prepared" for a meeting? What would it take to win the next meeting you are in?

ACTION Put together a two-page document for the next important meeting you attend.

39 Rigid goals are fragile goals.

Rigid goals aren't sustainable.

Rigid goals don't last.

Rigid goals aren't fun.

Rigid goals force you to white-knuckle your way through some sort of painful plan to change your life.

Want a sign your goal is becoming too rigid? I'll actually give you two, because I'm generous.

Your goal is too rigid if:

1. You become angry when someone interrupts it.
2. You beat yourself up if you miss it.

If your plan is to walk around your neighborhood every morning, and one day you can't because your child forgot their lunch at home, which forces you to drive to school to deliver it, keep an eye on your anger. If you're enraged at the audacity of that child and act as if they purposely forgot their lunch to ensure you never lose those extra pounds, be careful. Rigid goals hate it when people interrupt them and see any intrusion as a personal attack.

Likewise, if you miss your goal for a day or even weeks and your first response is to beat yourself up, be careful. Rigid goals are terrible at forgiving missed moments. They deal in shame and will be quick to heap a lot on you.

Be diligent with your goals. Work hard. Stretch beyond your comfort zone, but beware of rigid goals.

Rigid goals are fragile goals. Finishers are always flexible.

QUESTION Have you ever tried to do a goal "too perfectly"? What happened when you missed a day?

ACTION If you have only one way to do a goal (e.g., "I always walk for exercise"), come up with two alternatives ("I do jumping jacks when it's raining" or "I practice doing the stairs inside my house").

40 Criticism that costs nothing is worth nothing.

Criticism is sticky. It's easy to believe, easy to remember, and easy to repeat to ourselves internally.

Compliments, on the other hand, slide right off like water off a duck's back. We tend to ignore those as fast as we receive them. Recognizing that, it would be easy to say, "Screw the haters!" or "Ignore all criticism!"

That's the type of rhetoric that helps you build an Instagram account with motivational photos, but it's not great advice. Not everyone who disagrees with you is a hater. Sometimes they are just someone with a different opinion. Discourse in our country died the day we decided that if I disagree with you, it means I hate you.

And not all criticism is toxic. Some of it is actually good for you. Some feedback is extremely healthy. How do you tell the difference between the poisons and the vitamins?

One way is to ask what it cost someone to give you that feedback.

The problem right now is that most criticism doesn't cost the critic anything. Any stranger can drop a devastating comment about you in an Instagram post in thirty seconds. That didn't cost them anything, but you'll think about it for hours, maybe even days. That costs you a lot. Let's change that with a soundtrack.

Criticism that costs nothing is worth nothing.

The angry tweet from a stranger? That's 140 characters. That costs nothing and is worth nothing.

The Facebook comment full of hate? That took ten seconds. That costs nothing and is worth nothing.

The backstabbing gossip from a coworker in the break room? That costs nothing and is worth nothing.

If a close friend takes you to coffee and gives you feedback on something they're concerned about in your life, there's a cost. They have to be brave enough to tell you. They take the risk that you'll overreact. They've given you hours, if not days, of their time as they thought about the issue. It costs them a lot and is therefore worth a lot.

If the feedback costs the critic something, it's probably worth something. They might be giving you a gift instead of just cutting you down. If it costs them nothing, though, its value is nil, so move on quickly.

Criticism that costs nothing is worth nothing.

QUESTION | How well do you usually handle criticism? When was the last time you received some helpful criticism?

ACTION | Write down any worthless criticism you've been carrying around for too long and let it go.

41 I don't hold grudges against myself.

Do you have an archnemesis? I don't, but it seems like all my favorite superheroes do.

Batman has Joker.

Superman has Lex Luthor.

Even Dorothy has the Wicked Witch of the West.

I don't have a villain I'm actively warring against, but recently I realized I was holding a grudge against someone. Have you ever held a grudge? Maybe there was a coworker you couldn't stand or a neighbor you got into a fence war with or a relative that makes Thanksgiving unbearable? My grudge wasn't against any of those people. My grudge was against myself.

That's what happens when regret goes unchecked. For a few years, I regretted a career decision I made. I didn't deal with it. I didn't process it, learn a few lessons, and then move on. I just replayed it again and again. I mentally relived the dumb thing I did so often that I got mad. I was no longer remorseful, I was angry at the me I used to be. I blamed my current circumstances on him and used him as a scapegoat for why I couldn't make different decisions.

"If only I hadn't done that!" I thought. "How could I have been so blind?"

That's a silly way to live though. I don't want to hold a grudge against the person I spend the most time with. Imagine if I told you my archnemesis was me. What a conflicted, unproductive way to go through life that would be.

Never hold a grudge against yourself. The faster you can forgive the past you, the sooner the present you can start building the future you. Superman might have needed an archnemesis, but you don't. He also wore his underwear on the outside, so we probably shouldn't follow his lead for most decisions in life.

QUESTION | What's a regret in your life that it's time to retire?

ACTION | Forgive yourself for that thing you did, even if you knew better when you did it.

42 Assume they're busy too.

That friend you texted who didn't text you back is busy.

That coworker who didn't respond to the email you sent is busy.

The child you called who didn't return your voicemail is busy.

The neighbor you expected a thank-you note from after they borrowed your lawnmower is busy.

I could play this game all day with every single person you know, because every single person on the planet is busy. The problem is that we know *we* are, but we forget others are too. Animosity grows in small moments like that.

We know we didn't respond to that important text from a friend because we received it when we were desperately trying to get the kids out the door for Little

League practice. One cleat was missing, the Gatorade had already spilled, and that week's favorite T-shirt had tragically not been washed yet. We got a text in the middle of a hurricane and gave ourselves copious amounts of grace for not responding.

But our friend who didn't reply immediately? Surely they ignored our text for some deeply personal, deeply nefarious reason. How could they be so inconsiderate?

Or maybe they're busy too.

This soundtrack will reduce the relationship issues you have by about 42 percent. That's pretty good for only four words.

I guess I could have written a longer chapter explaining this, but I think you get the idea. And it turns out that I'm busy too.

QUESTION Have you ever overreacted when someone didn't respond to you quickly?

ACTION Follow up with the person you are waiting for a response from.

43 The early bird gets everything.

We used to camp a lot when we were first married. I thought it was because we loved the outdoors. Jenny clarified that for me and said it was mostly because we were poor. The only place we could sleep was outside. It cost $11 a night, which was about our entire vacation fund.

I remember those days fondly, in part because that's when I first learned the soundtrack "The early bird gets everything." I tend to be late to most situations. My internal clock came preset to last-minute. I did not grow up with the attitude that early is on time. That all changed with camping.

Campsites tend to come in two varieties: awesome and awful. The awesome ones are usually against the lake, the creek, or the woods. The road leading into the campground creates a cul-de-sac, with all the best sites on the outside of the loop. The ones in the middle of the cul-de-sac are the worst. It's like sleeping on a patch of grass in a Best Buy parking lot. You don't have a view, there aren't any trees, and you're exposed to every other campsite. There's zero privacy and zero charm. You are a "middle camper," meaning your poor little tent is set up in the middle of the campground chaos.

Do you know how to get the best campsites? You register early. Three months before middle campers are even thinking about going, you register the best site. In some situations, like national parks, you have to stay up until midnight a year before to register the days you want. True campers do it because they know that soundtrack you need to know too: "The early bird gets everything."

The best campsites. The best rides at Disney. The best table at the restaurant. The best class schedule at college. The best toys at Christmas. The best antiques at the estate sale. The best seats at the concert.

The world is built to accommodate and reward the early bird. That's not how I'm naturally wired, but eventually I just got tired of the leftovers. I don't want the best of what's left—I want the best. If you do, too, be the early bird. You get much more than just some gross worms. You get everything.

QUESTION | Does being early come easy for you, or is it a challenge?

ACTION | Plan something that's a month out and watch how much better it goes.

44 I keep promises to myself.

This week I'm too busy to write.

I have too many other commitments to go for a run.

Work is too hectic to take a walk with my wife.

Travel makes it too difficult to eat healthy.

I'm too tired to talk to my neighbor at the mailbox, even though I know how much community matters.

All of those things are true, and yet . . . there's a soundtrack that keeps me going:

I keep promises to myself.

That's the trick about goals. A goal is never just a goal. Goals are promises you make to yourself, and every time you break one, it gets easier to break the next one. Eventually you completely lose trust in yourself. The reason we're often filled with doubt about what we're capable of is because we've heard it all before. You start a new diet and immediately think, "Here we go again."

The good news is that this situation is 100 percent reversible. All you have to do is start keeping small promises to yourself. Like finding time to write even during a busy week. Running in between all the commitments. Walking with your wife after dinner. Bringing healthy snacks to the airport instead of pretending 9:45 a.m. is a reasonable time to eat a double cheeseburger just because your flight won't land until after lunch. Taking a few minutes to talk to the neighbor who you didn't know lost his job.

If you've broken the same promise a dozen times, maybe it's time to make the promise smaller. You could be trying something too big too soon. Keeping small promises to yourself makes keeping the next big one easier.

Make the goal. Honor the promise. Isn't that just what you and I do?

We keep promises to ourselves.

QUESTION | What's a promise to yourself that you keep breaking?

ACTION | Make the promise even smaller.

45 Busy beats bored.

When I was in high school, I worked at a store called Maurice the Pants Man. We sold pants. Maurice was crazy about them.

If you spend a single day working in retail, you learn a universal soundtrack that actually applies to every job:

Busy beats bored.

The days that were busy went by the fastest. A shift spent helping moms get back-to-school clothes for their grumpy teenage boys ("Mom, I only wanna wear shorts!") flew by. The afternoon shifts at Christmas were a blur. The rush leading up to Valentine's Day—just kidding, no one buys pants for that special someone.

Busy days were fast days.

The slow days were a drag. The days that felt like weeks were the days when I wasn't busy. Those days were torture because I didn't have enough to do. Years later, I would find out the same was true in corporate America. Though we often complain that being busy is a bad thing, it's not. I'll take a busy day over a boring one any day. I've had jobs that were so dull that I sometimes felt like I finished the internet. Have you ever felt that way? Like you already surfed so much that there was nothing new on the internet? Ugh, that's the worst.

The next time you're tempted to complain that your life is so busy, pause for a second. Aren't you glad it is? Aren't you glad your kids have lots of commitments, you have more friends than you can possibly catch up with, and work believes in you so much that they've filled your schedule to capacity? I am.

Busy beats bored.

QUESTION Have you ever complained about being too busy? What if it all went away instantly? What would you miss?

ACTION Plan one extra activity you could add to your schedule this week.

46 Do both.

I get a lot of "or" questions from people.

Should I go to college *or* get a job?

After college, should I get a job *or* a master's degree?

Should I start a side hustle *or* work for someone?

Should I volunteer more *or* get in shape?

Should I write my book *or* pay off my debt?

My answer is always the same: Do both.

You have more to give than you can possibly imagine. It's human nature to think you're close to running out of time, energy, and ability. If people have ten gears, they will tell you that they are operating at gear 8. They are not. They are at gear 5, at best. This isn't hyperbole. I did a research study with Mike Peasley, PhD. More than 50 percent of the people in the study admitted that 50 percent of their full potential was untapped. They were operating at half capacity. Do you know what you could accomplish with 50 percent more? I do—both!

I'm not a full-time writer. That's a fun fantasy, but it's really not true. In most years, more than 80 percent of my overall income is not from books. I'm a public speaker. I teach online courses. I host a podcast. I coach people. I throw live events. I sell merchandise. I sometimes think it would be easier if I could quit everything, move to the Pacific Northwest, and write a book in a quiet cabin. Maybe, but then I would miss the immense joy of public speaking, leading a company, and the thousand other things I do in an average week.

Plus, I'm capable of doing both.

You are too.

We just solved the next difficult choice you have to make. When you face a fork in the road, do both.

QUESTION What is one area of life you know you're capable of more?

ACTION One of your friends is already doing both. Ask them how they're doing it.

47 My idea isn't as crazy as the Bubba Gump Shrimp Co.

I'm not worried about your idea.

You might think it won't work.

You might think it's silly, dumb, or too late to do it.

You might lose confidence in your idea from time to time.

You might be worried about your idea, but I'm not.

Why?

Because Bubba Gump Shrimp Co. is still in business.

Just so we're clear, it's a seafood restaurant themed after a movie that came out in 1994. That concept is more than thirty years old and it's still going. A supporting character in a movie dreamed of a fictional shrimp company that now has more than thirty locations, including three in Japan and one in Hong Kong. They serve seven million people a year. At this very moment there is a man in Japan enjoying the Shrimper's Net Catch with Mama Gump's Garlic Bread Basket. I refuse to believe your idea is crazier than that.

If it is, I'd like to remind you that someone once said in a meeting, "Let's make a film with a tornado full of sharks." Then they did and the franchise made a reported $789 million.

I promise your idea has a better shot than that concept did.

QUESTION Are you as surprised as I was that Bubba Gump Shrimp Co. still exists?

ACTION Make a list of three other crazy, successful ideas as a reminder of what's possible for the next time you worry about your own idea.

48 I am my biggest investor!

In 2011, I wrote a book called *Quitter: Closing the Gap Between Your Day Job and Your Dream Job*. I had fun writing it, but lots of people hated the first chapter. The reason was simple. The title is "Don't quit your day job."

Some readers picked it up hoping I would tell them just the opposite. "Quit today! Throw caution to the wind! Your day job is holding you back!"

But what if it's not? What if your day job is the only thing standing between you and every hungry bill you have? What if your day job is the only thing keeping the lights on, your car running, and your kids fed?

It's popular to demonize our day jobs as dream snatchers, but today's soundtrack isn't going to do that. In fact, this is the opposite of everything you've been taught about corporate America, but I still want you to say it.

I am my biggest investor!

If you have a dream job you'd rather be doing right now but it's not ready yet, guess what is funding that pursuit? Your day job! It's not holding you back—on the contrary, it's investing in your future. When I was a corporate copywriter but wanted to be a public speaker, my day job paid for my ability to travel to events that weren't paying me yet. It allowed me to hire a professional designer to build my website. It bought stickers and T-shirts I could hand out to readers of my blog.

I was my biggest investor!

If you repeat that soundtrack and look at your day job that way, every single day of work will get better. Instead of being bothered by all the tasks you have to do when you'd rather be at your dream job, you will see how the two are connected. One is paying for the other.

Don't fight your day job—embrace it.

You are your biggest investor.

QUESTION Do you love what you do for a living? Would you like to do something else in the future?

ACTION Write down three things your job allows you to do outside of your job (e.g., vacation, braces for my kids, business license for my side hustle).

49 Put your motion where your mouth is.

Your spouse is going to clap when they read this soundtrack. Your friends will let loose a holler. Your boss might even cheer a bit. You won't like this soundtrack at first, but you'll love it as soon as it starts working.

In my mid-thirties, I had a lot of dreams but very few actions. I was quick to tell everyone all the amazing things I was going to do someday. You just watch out—I am going to take it to the next level! I'll write books. I'll start a business. I'll run races and get in shape. I'll build the kind of epic life I know I am capable of! Someday.

I had ten thousand words and zero actions.

That puts everyone you know in a difficult spot.

They want to support you. Your significant other wants to root for you. Your friends want to show up for you. Your boss wants to see you excel at work. (Even a grumpy boss knows that when you get great at your job, it makes their life easier.)

But actions are easier to support than words.

Jenny could read my manuscript to give me feedback, but not until I wrote it.

My friend Rob could cheer for me at a half marathon, but not until I ran it.

My coworker Bill could support me in a client presentation, but not until I gave it.

People love supporting your actions—they're tired of hearing your words. That feels a bit like tough love, but it's time you and I get busy.

It might not be time to put your money where your mouth is, but it's always time to put your motion where your mouth is.

Want more support for your goals and dreams? Actions are easier to support than words. Put your motion where your mouth is.

? QUESTION | What dream do you talk about the most? Have you ever wanted more support from the people you know?

ACTION | Take one action toward that dream today.

50 I'm not where I want to be yet, but I'm not where I was.

If you don't know who originally said a soundtrack, you can just attribute it to Abraham Lincoln, Winston Churchill, or Mother Teresa. They are quoted constantly, so maybe that's where this one comes from. I don't know its origin, but I do know I cling to it like a piece of driftwood in a storm.

This is a refocusing soundtrack, meaning that it takes your gaze off one thing and puts it on another. Instead of looking at what consultant Dan Sullivan calls "The Gap," the distance between you and your goal, you look at "The Gain," how far you've come from your starting point.

It's human nature to do the opposite. We have an eye for what's missing, not what's been achieved. That's why a parent can look at the one B on a report card full of A's and ask their kid what happened in that class.

The best part of this soundtrack is that it strikes the perfect balance between honesty and hopefulness.

You don't fix an old lie with a new lie. That's why so many people don't trust motivational content. If I told you to say, "I'm exactly where I want to be today, and I'm already perfect," you'd know I wasn't telling the truth. You're not there—me either.

Honesty is saying, "I'm not where I want to be yet, but I'm not where I was." And there's hope built into this honesty.

The first burst of it is in the word "yet." Few words are this small and this powerful. "Yet" says it's going to happen. "Yet" says it's coming. "Yet" says it's not impossible.

The second wave of hope is in the simple statement "I'm not where I was." You're not. Even if the gain is small, it's there. Even if it feels impossible to see sometimes, it's there. You're not where you were. You've made progress.

Don't give up. Take small steps. Don't stare at how far you have to go—look at how far you've come.

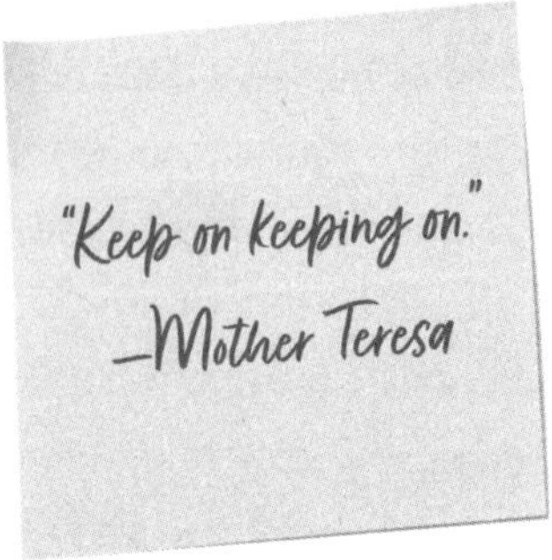

QUESTION When do you feel most discouraged about your progress? When do you feel most encouraged?

ACTION Come up with one simple way to measure your progress. For example, use the Strava app to track your steps, cross off days to a goal on your calendar, or put marbles in a jar every time you complete an action.

51 I wonder what that means?

I love Crazy Aaron's Thinking Putty. If you've never seen it before, imagine if Jell-O was also a fidget spinner. It's colorful putty that comes in dozens of shapes and styles in beautifully designed metal tins. They sell it at toy stores, but it's the kind of kid product that is secretly for adults.

I bought some one afternoon while out with my family in Boone, North Carolina. As we walked down the street with my fresh, admittedly silly purchase, I told my oldest daughter, "I can't wait to use this stress putty when I get home to finish writing my new book."

Without missing a beat she said, "Dad, you keep calling it stress putty. That's not the name. The name is *thinking* putty." She was right. I wasn't using the correct word. There's a huge difference between thinking and stressing. Later that night, when I was reflecting on that moment, I thought about one of my favorite soundtracks: "I wonder what that means?"

Self-awareness is a superpower. It's nearly impossible to change your life if you don't know what's really going on. But how do you build self-awareness in practical ways? You use simple soundtracks like this:

I wonder what that means?

When you bump into something about yourself that surprises you, ask that question. In this example, instead of using the word "thinking" I was using the word "stress." They are not the same. I was acting like thinking is always stressful. I wonder what that means?

One afternoon, when a podcast host emailed me to check that I had a good mic before our interview, I got really angry. My ego welled up in me. *You don't think I have a microphone? You think I'm such an amateur that I don't even own a microphone? How dare you!*

Whoa, what? They didn't say any of that. I wonder what that means?

When your response to a situation is unusual, inappropriate, or surprising, bust out this soundtrack. Then be brave enough to pull the thread a bit to see what's really going on.

If that feels challenging, you should get some thinking putty. See? I used the correct name. I'm already making progress.

? QUESTION | What's the last time your reaction to a comment or situation surprised you?

ACTION | Ask the question "I wonder what that means?" at least once today. Sit with the answer for a few minutes.

52 The fastest way to get encouraged is to encourage someone else.

Is this a soundtrack or a life hack? Yes.

If you want to feel instantly encouraged, just encourage someone else. Maybe you're thinking, *No, no, no, Jon, I think you misheard me. I'm the one who is discouraged. I'm the one who needs encouragement from somebody.* I know—me too most days. But I promise, the not-so-secret way to feel better is to make someone else feel better first.

Don't believe me? Try this simple experiment:

1. Criticize a friend.
2. Encourage a friend.

Make a mental note of which made you feel better. When you walked away from those two interactions, which one left a lingering feeling of overall grossness? Which one made you feel lighter? I bet I know the answer.

This soundtrack flat out works, and I use it *all* the time—even in unexpected places like the airport. If you're not a business traveler, you probably think the airport is a magical place that whisks you away to vacations. Not for me. It's where I go to get delayed, canceled, and verbally assaulted by overheard announcements about the gentleman who left his iPad at TSA.

That's why when I walk through the airport, I make a point of complimenting strangers. At least once a trip, I find someone with bright green shoes or polka dot glasses and say, "Those are really working for you! Those are great." I tell people with dogs, "That's an awesome dog!" I find someone in a Boston Celtics jersey and tell them, "Jayson Tatum doesn't get the respect he deserves!" (I grew up in Massachusetts.)

They always light up with the unexpected encouragement, and so do I.

If you see me in an airport, feel free to tell me you like Larry Bird too, my shoes are cool, or my suitcase game is on point (it is). We could probably both use a little encouragement.

QUESTION | What's another hack you've found to bring your spirits up when you feel discouraged?

ACTION | Give one compliment to a complete stranger today.

53 Kids are resilient, but they'd rather not be.

"Kids are resilient." We hear that a lot. We say it after they've been through tragedy. It's meant to encourage us that they'll be OK. They can bounce back. They'll make it through this.

It's true, kids are resilient, but only because they have to be. Given the option, they'd prefer to be safe. They'd rather be protected. They'd rather have stable homes and happy parents and friends to sit with at lunch.

What do you do with that? It depends on who is reading this right now. Maybe for you it means drinking less or not at all. Maybe it means going to counseling so that your anger issues become a thing of the past. Maybe it means sending your kids to therapy so that they can process whatever is going on for them right now. Maybe it means not taking that promotion so you can be at more of their games. Or maybe it's the exact opposite and you need to take a second job to put out the financial fires that are stressing out your whole family, including your kids.

This soundtrack should have come with a warning label (or at least some thinking putty) because it's so serious. Don't get discouraged though—kids *are* resilient. Now, as adults, let's figure out some simple ways for them not to need so much resilience. They've got the rest of their lives to need to bounce back. Just wait until they find out about taxes and the DMV.

Let's keep kids kids as long as we can.

QUESTION If you're a parent, how could you encourage your kid today?

ACTION Give yourself a little credit for the last situation you bounced back from. Turns out you're resilient too.

54 Half in is all out.

This week I rented an office on main street in Franklin, Tennessee.

Why? Half in is all out.

This week I posted my goals publicly to more than five hundred people in the Remarkable You Community.

Why? Half in is all out.

This week I planned every workout in my calendar ahead of time.

Why? Half in is all out.

Partial dreams come with partial benefits.

You also quit by week two. That's not an exaggeration, that's data. Strava, one of the world's largest fitness tracking apps, analyzed 31.5 million athletic activities to determine when people quit their New Year's resolutions. Know what they found? The largest drop-off is the second Friday of January. Most people don't even make it to February!

As I said back in chapter 27, though, we're not most people.

It's hard to half swim, one foot on the shore, one foot in the ocean. It's hard to half write, one hand on the keyboard, the other behind your back. It's hard to half present to a new client on Zoom, one side of your face in the meeting, the other side watching TV. All in is a lot more productive and ultimately a lot more fun.

Let's be honest, it's scary. The "all in" do get a few more bruises. They get a few more bumps. They need a few more Band-Aids for the scrapes that always come with adventures, but that's OK. They also get all the rewards, all the prizes, all the glory, and all the satisfaction.

Half in is all out.

Are you all in?

QUESTION | What part of your life do you feel like you're holding back?

ACTION | Pick one small goal you can go all in on today.

55 Easy is a clue.

If someone ever asks you to make a balloon arch for a party, say no. Don't even think about it for a second—just give an immediate "no thanks." Those things might look good on an Instagram post, but I assure you they are impossible to build. By the end of the experience you won't even want to go to the party, you'll probably stop speaking to your friend, and for the rest of your life you'll be triggered every time you see a balloon.

There's only one caveat to this very helpful advice: unless it's easy for you to build balloon arches.

Maybe you're a pro, maybe you've made a hundred of them in your lifetime, maybe you're a natural. If you are, I bet when someone compliments you about that skill, you say what most people say: "That? Oh, that's nothing. It's easy."

We tend to discount and dismiss things that are easy to us. Humor is easy to me. I grew up in a funny family. I'm currently raising a funny family. I thought every kid's dad brought them to comedy clubs when they were young. Making people laugh is easy.

That's not bragging. That's a clue to one of life's biggest mysteries: *What's my purpose?*

That's a huge question, isn't it? We all want to find our purpose and our why. What if it's very obvious and has just been hidden behind the curtain of "easy"? We often think that only difficult things have value. That's a broken soundtrack that has cost many people their best gifts.

The next time someone compliments you for an achievement, don't assume it's easy. It might be for you, but the rest of us think it's amazing. My accountant Pam thinks federal taxes are easy. They're not to me. My friend Jason thinks glaucoma surgery is easy—he performs thirty of them a day. They're not easy to me. My coworker Chris thinks selling sponsorships to events is easy. They're not to me.

Pay attention to what comes easy to you. Imagine if you found a way to do more of that in your career. Do you know what you'd say every day after work? "That was easy."

QUESTION | What comes easy to you? (Don't say Netflix—you know what I mean!)

ACTION | Today, give a compliment to a friend who makes something look easy.

56 Everything is always working out for me!

This one is a James Victore original. He's an author, painter, designer, and business coach extraordinaire. When I hired him one year to help me get unstuck, he taught me this soundtrack, and it immediately became a mainstay in the Acuff house.

My poor kids are sick of hearing me say this over and over again.

When I get the last standby seat on a flight home, I say, "Everything is always working out for me!" If Dairy Queen makes too many Blizzards and gives us an extra one for free, I say, "Everything is always working out for me!" If my publisher decides to translate one of my books into Romanian, I say, "Everything is always working out for me!" When I have big victories, small wins, and everything in between, I say this soundtrack. I love it so much I already wrote about it in the original *Soundtracks* book.

So then why am I writing about it again? Because it works.

I sold more than 250,000 copies of that book, and this is one of the soundtracks people tell me about the most. Want to know why?

Because it improves your eyesight. It's like getting Lasik for your attitude. It makes it so much easier to see the good in your day.

It's not magic. I don't win every situation. I lose an awful lot. But when I say this soundtrack, it fixes my eyes on the good things. It changes my vision toward the positive. I can already see the negative. It's easy to find the failures. But the good stuff? That takes work—and most importantly, that takes a fire soundtrack.

This is the one.

Thanks for sharing it with me, James.

I'm glad that out of all ten million business coaches on the internet I found you, but I'm not surprised. Why?

Because everything is always working out for me!

? QUESTION

Is it easier for you to spot the good things in life or the bad? How could you look on the bright side a little more?

ACTION

Apply this soundtrack to three good things (of any size!) that happen to you today.

57 What don't I know?

Luci Swindoll, a prolific writer and speaker, used to carry a note in her pocket that read, "They might be right." It was her way of having patience with people who had different opinions from her. Maybe they were right.

I've never carried that same note, but I did learn to ask a question after completely misreading a coworker twenty years ago. I'll call him Scott and say that he was from Texas, because two decades later I am still a little embarrassed about my behavior and I don't want him to know I'm writing about him.

Scott and I worked together in a marketing department for a big company. In Texas. Let's pretend it was Buc-ee's because that makes the story cooler. I couldn't stand Scott. He was rude. He was dismissive. He was constantly late. He was never focused on his work and made my job difficult.

Then I found out his wife had cancer.

Everything changed in that moment. Now I knew that he wasn't rude because he was a jerk but because he was terrified that his wife was going to die. He wasn't dismissive because he didn't care about the work but because he was hyperfocused on making it through the next round of chemo. He wasn't late because he was lazy. He was late because he was caring for a sick spouse. He wasn't unfocused. He was busy thinking about his wife's cancer.

Humans are fantastic at judging people. Maybe that goes back to our cave-dweller days, when a dark shape we thought was a bush would actually be a saber-toothed tiger and we'd be dead. I'm not sure. I just know that in every situation, there's something I don't know. You too.

What if you used that soundtrack the next time you were tempted to make a snap judgment about a coworker, family member, or friend?

What don't I know?

I bet it's a whole lot and you'll be glad you paused to get a little more information.

(PS: Can you believe I used to work at Buc-ee's in Texas? That beaver mascot? My idea.)

QUESTION Who is one person you've judged too quickly in the past without knowing the whole story?

ACTION Grab a sticky note and write "What don't I know?" on it. Put it somewhere you'll see it daily.

58 Success is the goal.

"Cheap is cool" is a soundtrack that my friend's family used to say. They made a point of always buying the most inexpensive option, even if it meant the item broke in a matter of weeks and they had to buy five replacements. This was my shoe plan, too, until I got married.

I used to buy horrendous $40 shoes for work that would fall apart in a few months. My wife, who did not have the many broken soundtracks about money that I did, finally said, "It's time to buy a nice pair of shoes." So I did. They cost $300. I've worn them for the last six years.

They felt extra expensive at the time because, like a lot of people, I thought poverty was noble. I believed that the only way to get ahead in life was to cheat or steal from others. Life was a pie with a fixed number of pieces. If I was successful and my piece got bigger, then surely I took that from someone else and should feel ashamed.

The only way to feel OK was to make sure I kept my finances under some arbitrary amount. Rich people were dishonest. The poor were noble. Gotcha.

Have you ever met someone who crawled their way out of real poverty though? They do not hold it in some sort of false esteem like middle-class people do. Carol Foderick, one of Toronto's top real estate agents, told me, "My childhood wasn't the *Coal Miner's Daughter*, where 'we were poor, but we did have love.' That's a myth. People living in real poverty are often surrounded by addiction and abuse."

It's not noble. It's not something to aspire to. It's something to help others out of, including yourself. It's a lot harder to do that when you're listening to broken soundtracks about money. It took me years to realize there's more than enough pie for everyone and that success is a worthy reward for hard work. Sometimes I still catch myself slipping back into my old ways. I recently realized I was refusing to call my assistant "my assistant" because I didn't want to brag. What? I have an executive assistant because I am an executive. Who was I worried would shame me for that expense?

Success is the goal. Success is the goal. Success is the goal.

I hope you own nice shoes. I hope you build an empire that employs dozens of people like Carol did. I hope you never mythologize poverty and use the phrase "must be nice" to describe someone more accomplished than you. It *is* nice—for them and maybe even for you someday if you start listening to better soundtracks about money.

QUESTION What's a soundtrack your parents said about money? Does it encourage or discourage you?

ACTION Think of something you want but have been telling yourself you "shouldn't" spend money on. If it's within your budget, go buy it right now—no guilt allowed. If you can't afford it, start saving today.

59 Small steps stack.

I spent 1,000 hours outside in 2024. Not in a row, which would have been an epic 41-day camping trip. I can't even begin to calculate how many bug bites I'd get in that length of time.

I spent 1,000 hours outside over the entire year. That doesn't sound like a big deal until you think about how little time you spend outside in an average day. Before I started using the app 1,000 Hours Outside that Ginny Yurich created, I bet I only spent thirty minutes a day outside.

Think about it: You drive to work inside a car. You eat lunch inside at your desk or at a restaurant. You have dinner inside. You watch TV inside. You go to bed inside. Unless you take a walk after dinner, there's not a lot of outside time built into an ordinary day.

In order to hit my goal, I needed to spend about three hours of every day outside. That is when I discovered the power of the soundtrack "Small steps stack." On most days, it was difficult to find three consecutive hours to be outside. Imagine telling your boss, "I'm going to take all my meetings outside today. Just crack a window and I will try to hear what you guys are saying." That wouldn't work. Would you hug your family after dinner and say, "I'll be in the backyard from seven to ten tonight if you need me"? That's weird too.

Instead of three-hour chunks, I had to find fifteen- and thirty-minute segments that would add up over time. I would take the occasional phone call meeting on a walk and pick up half an hour. I'd answer emails outside for fifteen minutes. I'd talk my family into dinner on the back porch some nights and grab another forty-five minutes. Those times didn't seem like much, but small steps stack. It worked so well that I started applying it to other parts of my life.

Why will you find me walking a mile in an airport? Because I have a walking goal, and even though I'd prefer to take a five-mile hike in the woods, a two-hour layover in Atlanta is what I have to work with. Better get moving.

Perfectionism tells you that life is all or nothing, meaning you should accomplish the whole three hours at once or not even bother. That's not true. Small steps stack. If you've got a big goal, slice it down to impossibly small steps. Walk in the airport. Take a phone call outside. Save $20 a pop even if your goal is to save $1,000. Over the course of a month, year, or lifetime, those small steps really do add up.

QUESTION What's the smallest amount of progress you can make on a goal you care about?

ACTION Start with ten minutes. That's all. Give a goal you're working on ten minutes today.

60 More goals, fewer rules.

Have you ever read a book to your kids and realized it is actually for adults too? It has a universal message that applies to everyone. This soundtrack is exactly like that.

It began one summer when my wife and I discovered two things:

1. Our kids were on their phones a lot.
2. They weren't reading many classic books at school.

The temptation in moments like that is to create rules: You can only use your phone sixty minutes a day! No video games until your chores are finished. You have to read forty-five minutes every night after dinner.

I'm not against rules, I just remember that as a kid, the more rules I had, the more I was tempted to break them. I wasn't rebellious, but the more restrictions that were placed on my adolescence, the more I wanted to push back against them.

Goals are different. Goals give kids something to aspire to, not suffocate under. To fix our summer, we paid our kids to read fifteen classic books. They helped pick the books, and we made it worth their while financially. It wasn't an allowance—it was good money paid for good work.

I knew it was working when I saw my youngest daughter reading *The Count of Monte Cristo* by the pool while everyone else her age was on TikTok. She wasn't keeping the rules, she was reaching for a goal.

The best mentors I've ever had always set me a goal to reach for, not a rule to obey. One bought a house in Italy. I saw that and thought, "I'd like to do that someday!" That became a goal I looked up to. He didn't say, "Jon, the new rule is that you shouldn't waste money going out to dinner all the time." That would have made me want to go out even more! Instead, he just showed me what was possible when you are responsible with your money, and I wanted that! That changed my behavior, not a set of rules.

The Acuff house has plenty of rules, but I bet we have more goals than the average family. If you really want your family to build remarkable lives, remember this soundtrack:

More goals, fewer rules.

QUESTION What's one rule in your house that you could change into a goal?

ACTION Create a scorecard for the goal. It could be a calendar, a tally, a checklist, or an app. Make it visible for everyone in the house to see.

61 Fall in like with the achievement. Fall in love with the action.

It takes too long to write books.

I hate to burst your bubble if you're a would-be author, but it's true. It takes me about one thousand hours to write a book. That is an eternity! The even worse news is that the amazing feeling you have when you hold the finished manuscript for the first time lasts about only thirty minutes. The accomplishment of seeing it on a shelf lasts for about only ninety minutes. The warm buzz of someone telling you that they read the book lasts about thirty minutes.

Why do I keep doing it then?

Because I fell in like with the achievement, but I fell in love with the action.

The action is always longer than the achievement. When you finish a half marathon, you feel great the rest of the day, but it took you eight weeks of training to get there. The training is massive. The triumph is momentary. You have to find joy in the journey or you'll never reach the destination. I don't write books because I know at the end of the two-year experience I will get to feel a fleeting sense of accomplishment. I write books because I've learned how to love writing.

I don't wait two years to feel good—what a slog that would be! I feel good every time I sit down to write. Sure, some days are harder than others and the words don't come easy, but it's still a good day. It has to be, or else why go to all that trouble?

My friends who run ultramarathons don't do it for the crowds. There are none. They don't do it for the money. There isn't any. They don't do it for the accolades. No one cares that you ran a hundred miles in the woods, you weirdo. They do it because they've learned how to love the action of running.

Achievements are nice, and you should definitely like them. I do. But the real juice is in the action. When you fall in love with that, every day feels victorious.

QUESTION What's one action related to your current career that you could fall in love with?

ACTION Interview that action and identify the easiest part of it to fall in love with.

62 Stuff tells a story.

I don't want a new hiking backpack.

You might think I do based on my recent browsing history. I am all over REI. I've been camped out on Osprey's website looking at all their different options. I've watched YouTube reviews from outdoor enthusiasts who always live in Colorado. (It's hard to be a serious hiker if you live in Kansas.)

The algorithm would tell you that I am obsessed with backpacks, but I don't want one. What I really want is to be the kind of person who lives a life that requires a hiking backpack. I want adventures. I want vistas. I want the outdoors.

I want to need a backpack. I want to have friends who call me up for a last-second trip to the Smoky Mountains. I want to do long day hikes with my family where it's impossible for us to be on our phones because we're so far from a good cell signal. I want to meet a buddy after work and fill my backpack with weights so we can get an even harder hike in.

That's what I really want, not a backpack.

Stuff always tells a story.

The things we buy are rarely about the actual things. The things we want are tiny little windows into our hearts. The sports car is about feeling successful. The house is about feeling safe. The running shoes are about feeling fast. The purse is about feeling accepted by all the other women who are in the know too and have the same one.

I've mentioned self-awareness a few times already in this book. Want another quick way to learn about yourself?

Interview your most recent purchases.

What's the story they're telling you about you?

? QUESTION | What's the purchase you've been thinking about the most lately? You know the one—it's already in your cart but you just haven't clicked "Buy" yet.

ACTION | Remove that item from your cart unless it's a story you really believe in.

63 D stands for "developing."

I got a D-minus today and I was pretty excited about it. Before I learned how to use soundtracks, that sentence would have killed me, but I genuinely mean it. I bombed a goal this morning and I'm proud.

For weeks I've been ignoring the training sessions on my Garmin watch. An Apple Watch gives you warm encouragement throughout the day, celebrating even the tiniest bit of progress like the grandma who brought their favorite granddaughter to audition for *American Idol*. "Isn't she pretty? Voice like an angel!" A Garmin is just the opposite. It's like a drill sergeant who constantly yells at you.

Today it suggested that I run four different four-minute segments at a pace of 7:20 per mile. I usually run at about 9:20 per mile, so that was a lot faster than

I'm used to. Every time I would reject that suggestion, my watch would say something like, "Why won't you let me help you, Jon? This hurts me more than it hurts you. I'm not mad, I'm just disappointed." I finally gave in this morning and tried its suggested run. It was a disaster. The first segment was OK, but they got progressively worse. At the end of the workout, Garmin said, "Complete. 60% effort." Congratulations, lazy bones—you got a D-minus!

Why was I excited about that? Because perfectionism used to prevent me from even trying goals like that. Perfectionism has one rule: If you can't do it perfectly, don't do it at all. I knew it would be a mess, so I'd been avoiding it. A perfectionist would rather get a zero than a D-minus. But here's the problem: No one starts with an A-plus. We want to, of course. I'd love to be a natural at everything I do, but that's not how life works. Everyone starts with an F. Scratch that—everyone *brave* starts with an F.

I don't want D's. I really don't. But they're a lot easier to deal with if I understand what they really mean: *developing*. When I try something new and get a D, that means I am developing. I am in-process. I am on the first rung of a ladder. That's how ladders work. You never start at the top, always at the bottom.

The next time a smartwatch shames you or a project falls flat or a new diet has a few hiccups, remember: D stands for developing, and everyone brave starts with an F.

QUESTION Have you ever struggled with perfectionism? What helps you deal with it?

ACTION Go find something new you want to do and get a D-minus in it.

64 Let me get back to you on that.

My desperate need for people to like me makes it difficult for me to say no. I am a recovering people pleaser. One sign that you are too is that you say yes to whoever is standing in front of you without considering all the other commitments you've already made to everyone else in your life.

The most common solution to this is a soundtrack I bet you've heard before: "*No* is a complete sentence." The idea is that you just say no. There doesn't have to be an explanation or disclaimer. Just "no." It sounds nice in theory, but it doesn't work in the real world—and it definitely doesn't work for people pleasers.

You look like a complete psychopath if a neighbor asks you to come over for dinner and you just say "no." What happens next? You just stare directly into their eyeballs and let the silence between you build until it's deafening? Is that what you want in your driveway? A gunslinger's standoff because you were told "no" is a complete sentence?

That sounds terrible. Fortunately, I've found a much better soundtrack:

Let me get back to you on that.

It's the perfect soundtrack because it ends the request and buys you time to think. Maybe you would like to say yes. Maybe you really want to say no. In the moment, it's hard to tell. So pause, assess, and respond later.

The second part of this soundtrack is to respond via email or text. You're not breaking up with someone you dated in college and need to have a face-to-face heart-to-heart with. You're saying no to an inconvenient ask. Make it easy on yourself. When you do, don't leave the door cracked open with a promise of later. If you say, "I'm too busy right now," a persistent person will ask, "When is a better time?"

Keep your no short. Just say, "I thought some more about what we discussed, and I won't be able to do that. Thanks for the offer!" No open loops. No ambiguity about the future. Quick text, quick email, end of story.

Would you like to get together for coffee with me to talk about this soundtrack?

Let me get back to you on that.

QUESTION Is it hard for you to say no? What's the last thing you said yes to that you regretted?

ACTION Say "Let me get back to you on that" ten times out loud today to get used to how those words feel. The more you say it, the easier it will be to mean it the next time someone asks you to do something you don't want to do.

65 I don't know yet.

Everyone is a leader. If you manage people at work, that's easy to see, but there are so many other leadership opportunities that we don't give ourselves enough credit for.

If you have kids, you are a leader.

If you have friends, you are a leader.

If you have a job, you are a leader.

If you have parents, you are a leader.

It's true, as a mom or dad you are in a leadership role. As a friend, there are going to be moments where you have to lead your friends out of a crisis. The buddy who is going through a divorce or a health scare needs some leadership. At every job, even if you're at the bottom of the corporate ladder, you have to lead up. You have to manage the people above you. And eventually you even end up parenting your parents as they age.

Are you convinced? Good, because there's a soundtrack every leader needs in their arsenal:

I don't know yet.

The best leaders in the world say this constantly. Leadership doesn't mean you *have* all the answers. Leadership means you'll *get* the answers.

It would be impossible to have all the answers. There's too much information. There are more than two million books published every year. Have you read them all?

People can tell when a leader is making something up because they're afraid to admit they don't know. When you say "I don't know yet," you're being honest. You strengthen every relationship you have every time you tell the truth.

The second reason this soundtrack works is that "yet" implies that you'll figure that out. You're on it. You've got it. You don't know yet, but you will. Then you write down their question and get the answer. Leaders don't know all the answers, but they know how to find them.

Don't pretend you know everything. People don't like following pretenders. They like following leaders, and leaders are quick to say, "I don't know yet."

QUESTION | Who is the best leader you've worked with? What's one of their qualities you respect?

ACTION | Today, when someone asks you a question you can't answer, tell them, "I don't know yet."

66 Diamonds are complex. Rocks are simple.

My fifties are more complex than my twenties were. This surprised me initially because I thought one of the goals was for your life to get simpler as you got older. That hasn't happened for me.

My job is a lot more complex than it used to be. Running my own company has more challenges than when I was a junior copywriter at Staples. I could leave that stress at work each day because I had zero responsibility.

My family is more complex than it used to be. I'm caught between parenting my own adult children and taking care of my aging parents. (Dad, you know it's true. You're the most active seventy-five-year-old I know, but I didn't worry about you in my twenties like I do now.)

Retirement also now feels like a real thing that is going to happen to me, not just a far-off concern for old people. You ever try to save the right amount of money in the right way so that you pay the least amount of taxes when you're in your seventies? Complex.

Working out in your fifties is way more complicated than in your twenties. I didn't even know I had knees until my forties, and now I have to check in with them to see if I have permission to run that day.

Life is complex, but there's a soundtrack that helps me see the upside in that:

Diamonds are complex. Rocks are simple.

A brilliant diamond has fifty-eight different facets that reflect light. The complexity of the diamond is what makes it valuable. A stone that breaks in half only has one cut, and that's simple, but nobody wants that for their wedding.

The best things in life are always that way. Relationships are complex, but they're worth it. Owning a business is complex, but it's worth it. Leading a team is complex, but it's worth it. Chasing a dream is complex, but it's worth it. Writing a book is complex, but it's worth it.

I have a sneaking suspicion that my sixties are going to be more complex than my fifties, especially if I don't figure out how to take my dad's mountain bike away. I can't wait for my sixties to get here, though, because diamonds are complex and I want a life that's brilliant.

? QUESTION Does your life feel more complicated today than it was ten years ago? What would it take to see the value in that?

ACTION Write down three complicated parts of your life. Then write down one thing about each of them that you can be grateful for. And don't forget—you could have a boring rock instead.

67 Criticize. Cheer. Create.

Use this soundtrack every time you go online, because those are the three options you have.

The first is the easiest. Cynicism is free. You can pop on Instagram and drop a mean comment on someone's photo with less than thirty seconds of effort. You can be jealous of an influencer, frustrated at a friend, or quietly petty about a coworker.

The second option costs maturity because you have to celebrate someone. This one is more difficult than the first but feels a lot better. You also don't have to apologize as much. It can be as simple as hearting a post or as complex as doing your own reaction video to someone's content that you like.

The third option is the hardest (and scariest) but also the best. Put yourself out there. Share an original idea.

Take your time and create a video you're proud of. Write a thread on X about selling a product at your first farmers market. Start a YouTube channel to showcase your home remodel project. Start a Facebook community around your favorite hobby. Do an Instagram Live of the first song you learned on acoustic guitar. The barrier to entry has never been lower, but it costs what it has always cost: a little bit of bravery.

Social media is jam-packed with people doing that first option. There are fewer people doing option two and even fewer attempting option three. I've personally done all of them. I started my first blog in 2001, so I've been around the digital block.

Option one is never worth it.

Option two might change your day.

Option three might change your life.

You probably already picked up your phone while reading this chapter. If you just jumped online, remember: Criticize. Cheer. Create.

Which one will you pick?

? QUESTION What sets off your "petty radar"? Is it politics? Fake mom influencers with perfect kids who at the age of two already read Mandarin? News about your rival sports team? (I live in SEC football country.)

ACTION Delete social media from your phone for twenty-four hours.

68 It's easier with coffee.

What's easier? Everything.

That should be the tagline for coffee: "We make everything easier."

Why is this soundtrack in this book? Because it's one of the most common soundtracks you'll hear at the Acuff house. I used it just yesterday. There was a tax issue Jenny and I needed to discuss. I brought it up right before bed. You'd think after a quarter century of marriage I would know better.

Dear men reading this book, do not bring up a serious, complicated, math-based issue with your wife right before you turn off the light. You might as well say, "I'd like to ruin the odds of you sleeping well tonight—let's talk taxes!" Three sentences into doing just that, I caught myself. (Self-awareness for the win!) Instead, I asked,

"Would you rather do this with coffee tomorrow morning?" and Jenny nodded an emphatic "yes" from her side of the bed. "You're right," I replied. "It's easier with coffee."

Life is easier when you line up the activities that require maximum mental freshness with the times of day when . . . you have maximum mental freshness.

This applies in marriage, parenting, and even work. For parenting, the time frame is reversed but the principle is the same. I didn't expect to have deep, heartfelt conversations with my teenagers at seven o'clock on Saturday morning like I do with my wife. My daughters were much more talkative at 10 p.m. after a night out with friends. Jenny and I stayed up later during those seasons knowing that was their "coffee hour."

At the office, I don't do work that demands serious creativity on Fridays at 4 p.m. Why? My tank is low. Monday morning with a coffee sets us up for much greater success.

It's easier with coffee. If you're into tea, tweak this one a bit and say, "It's easier with tea." If you're one of those annoying people who don't drink either, change it even further: "It's easier with energy."

If you want a strong marriage, communicative kids, and happy coworkers, match the time to the task—and always bring coffee.

QUESTION | Did this one make you want a coffee? Me too.

ACTION | Identify the time of day you feel most productive and schedule an important task in that window.

69 Use it all!

Creativity is a renewable resource. The more you use, the more you'll have.

I often forget that, though, and hoard ideas so that I "don't run out." Have you ever felt that way? You might not write books, but everyone is creative. It's human nature to think we must be careful with the supply we have.

We save some for a rainy day. We play it safe when we know we're capable of more. We hold back on the song, the photo, the business idea, the garden, the poem, the video, the anything. We want to make sure we have some for later. But I'm here to tell you a handful of secrets:

There is no later.

Art you sit on rots.

More leads to more.

That last one is my favorite because I think it works for much more than just creativity.

More generosity leads to more generosity.

More kindness leads to more kindness.

More laughter leads to more laughter.

The only way to get more of the thing you want is to use up what you already have. You won't run out. I couldn't say that with any degree of authority on book two, but on book twelve I'll shout it from the rafters. In the immortal words of Steven Pressfield from his book *The War of Art*, "Don't cheat us of your contribution. Give us what you've got!"[5]

When you do, don't be surprised when you get more. Creativity—and most of the best things in life—is a renewable resource.

QUESTION | When was the last time you "held back"?

ACTION | Spend a few minutes today pursuing your favorite form of creativity.

70 If we're both wrong, we'll be wrong together.

One of my goals with this book was to make sure it didn't turn into a collection of quotes from other people. There are already enough of those. I wanted every soundtrack to be one I had used in my own life and seen thousands of other people benefit from too. In order to guarantee that, I wrote the majority of them. But today's was written by Al Andrews.

Al is a Nashville legend. He's a counselor who started the nonprofit Porter's Call, which offers free therapy to the musicians in this very musical city. If you get any country music stars or indie songwriters in a room and say his name, you will hear stories like, "Al saved my marriage," "Al helped me get sober," "When my album sold ten million copies, Al helped me survive the fame." In a stroke of genius, when Al retired in his seventies, Belmont University asked him to teach their music majors a class called "Prehab." How do you have a successful music career without needing rehab? Take the class.

Al was college roommates with my dad. He was at the hospital the night I was born, so it's no exaggeration to say he's known me my entire life. A few years back, I called him in the middle of a crisis. He listened intently, asked a few questions, and then gave me some advice. As the call began to conclude, he told me a soundtrack I still use with any friend who's facing a challenge:

"If we're both wrong, we'll be wrong together."

That's ultimately what every one of your friends wants to know: *I'm not going anywhere. This is a storm and I'm going to stand in it with you. This isn't the only time we can talk about this problem—it's the first of a thousand times we can.*

Al also didn't sugarcoat the situation. Despite my best intentions, despite all the wisdom I was seeking, despite what all the experts were telling me, I still might make the wrong decision. Life is not guaranteed. But I wouldn't be wrong alone. We'd be wrong together.

You'll get to say this soundtrack someday, maybe sooner than you think.

Just make sure you credit Al Andrews, even if you're not a famous country musician.

? QUESTION | Who is the first friend you call when life goes sideways? Which friend calls you first?

ACTION | If you're in a storm right now, call that friend. If you're not in a storm right now, take a deep breath and be grateful for that. We often forget to notice when the seas are calm.

71 Everything you own wants a forever home.

The best part about soundtracks is that they apply to every area of your life.

Soundtracks will help you build a stronger marriage.

Soundtracks will make it easier to talk with your kids.

Soundtracks will encourage you while you get in shape.

Soundtracks will lead to greater financial prosperity.

Soundtracks will even help you find your keys.

Hold up . . . what? It's true. Today's soundtrack is designed to do that and so much more.

"Everything you own wants a forever home."

This one took me fifteen years of marriage to understand, but I think you can knock it out in a matter of minutes. I'm not exaggerating—that's how long it took me to believe my wife that life would be so much easier if I always put my keys in the same drawer. For a decade and a half, I ran around the house in a panic every time I had to go somewhere. There were easily a dozen different places they could be, with the occasional surprise spot thrown in just to keep things spicy. ("They're on the dryer, Jon!"—Jenny Acuff)

But my keys wanted a forever home. They didn't like all that stress. They didn't enjoy not knowing where they were going to sleep each night. They wanted the comfort and security of a consistent resting place. I eventually gave in, and it was magical for both of us. I will never again waste minutes of my life looking for my keys. I also won't lose my AirPods. They wanted a home too. Guess where it is? Inside the AirPods case! Go figure. The second I remove them from my ears, home they go. My backpack has a home. The paper towels have a home. My running socks have a different home from my work socks. I'm like Oprah giving her audience members cars, except I'm handing out homes to inanimate objects.

Ridiculous? Maybe a little, but how's treating all your stuff like nomads working out for you? It's stressful, right? Come home, friend. Bring your keys with you.

QUESTION Have you ever lost your keys or your wallet? Is that a feeling you'd like to have more or less often?

ACTION Unless you're already a master at organization, start with one drawer and one item. Or better yet, start with your keys.

72 Today is the youngest I'll ever be!

Dear early fifties Jon,

It's me, the seventy-seven-year-old version of you. I'm writing you from twenty-five years in the future. I won't tell you who the president is, what type of car we're driving these days, or if we ever did grow that mustache we always talked about. We've got much bigger issues to discuss.

I need you to write down this soundtrack and stick it in dozens of places around your house:

Today is the youngest I'll ever be!

Because it is and I don't think that's hit you yet. There are too many mornings when you lie in bed and don't want to go run. There are too many weekends when you want to skip the hike with your wife and just doomscroll for hours. There are too many summers when you think the cross-country vacation would be too difficult to plan so you settle for what you've already done. There are too many evenings when you go to bed too early instead of staying late with your friends at the dinner party and talking deep into the night.

Don't wait.

It doesn't get easier later. It only gets harder.

These are the youngest knees you will ever have. This is the most energy you will ever have. This is the most pep in your step you will ever have. I say that not to discourage you. The seventies are awesome. Your grandkids are going to blow you away! This isn't a warning, it's a wake-up call.

Go for it. Don't put off a single thing for a single day. Make the most of these moments. Invest in relationships. Eat healthy so that our nineties feel great too. Ask Jenny out on a date this weekend. Chase down a thousand Frisbee throws with your kids. Jump on every plane for every trip you can get your hands on. Above all, get that sports car. You ever see an old man fold himself into one of those? It's not a great look.

Today is the youngest you'll ever be!

? QUESTION What do you think the seventy-seven-year-old you would say to you?

ACTION Look up a video on YouTube about the best stretches for people your age. The older you will thank you for the investment in flexibility.

73 What did your wisest friends say?

If you were about to make a big decision, I'd ask you this question and you would hate me a little bit. That's fair—you should. If you love your personal trainer at the gym, you don't have a very good personal trainer. They should push you beyond your comfort zone. They should make you do things you wouldn't normally do. They should ask hard questions.

This soundtrack is one such question, and I already know the answer: "I haven't asked them yet."

I only know that's the answer because it's the one I used to give when mentors asked me similar questions. If I was about to make a big decision, especially one I was excited about, I didn't want to ask my wise friends for advice.

What if they disagreed with my decision? What if they told me to think about it longer? What if they saw problems inside the opportunity and cautioned me that this is too good to be true?

I would rather find a cheerleader friend who always just says, "Hooray, you should do that!" and then make a rash decision I almost immediately regret. I did that for years, but I really don't want to do that anymore. I'm tired of impulsive decisions that blow up in my face.

I'm becoming a huge fan of wisdom later in life. It's true, the older you get, the less enjoyable dumb, avoidable consequences are. So now I make it a point to ask wise people for wise advice. How revolutionary.

It takes a little longer than just shooting from the hip. I often argue against the very advice I've asked for before accepting it. It's not a foolproof system. Even ten smart people can all be wrong. But I've never walked away from getting wise advice and thought, "I wish I hadn't sought that counsel."

The next time you face a big decision, imagine me sitting across from you in a coffee shop. I'm only going to ask you one question:

"What did your wisest friends say?"

QUESTION

Which is a bigger challenge for you: making impulsive decisions too quickly or overanalyzing and making decisions too slowly?

ACTION

Make a list of three to five of your wisest friends so that you have it ready to go for the next big decision you make.

74 There's treasure in the transitions.

How many transitions do you make every day?

I make about fifty. I know because I'm a goal nerd and I counted them.

From bed to bathroom, from bathroom to coffee, from coffee to journaling, from journaling to working out, from working out to shower, from shower to commuting to the office, from commuting to working, from working to meeting, from meeting to meeting to meeting to meeting. And that's only the first few hours of my day.

You're the same way, and if you're like me, there's treasure in the transitions. If I pay attention to the transitions and make them intentionally, I reclaim so much time in my day. If I don't, I lose all that gold.

For example, if I bring my phone to the transition from workout to shower, I lose fifteen minutes. What am I doing? Standing in the bathroom, waiting for the water to warm up, scrolling through Instagram. If I don't know the first thing I'm doing when I transition from my morning commute to the office, I lose fifteen minutes spinning through the emails that stacked up last night while I was asleep. If I don't know what I want to do during the transition between home and work, I lose thirty minutes.

That last one is how I learned this soundtrack. In 2009, I had an hour commute each way because I lived in Atlanta, and Atlanta hates you. It just does. For the first few years of my commute, I goofed off with those two hours, listening to sports radio, cursing the nineteen million other people who were on the road with me, and grumbling about the unfairness of it all.

When I got serious about goals and mindset in my mid-thirties, I realized I had two big, beautiful hours of free time every day. If I made use of the transition, I could really change my life. I started listening to audiobooks. I made phone calls to side hustle clients. I even practiced speeches out loud to my steering wheel as I drove. There was treasure in the transitions, and I wanted all of it.

You should too.

You're busy. So am I. But I guarantee there's a lot of treasure in your day that's just waiting to be found.

QUESTION What's the transition in your day that is hardest for you to make? What's one way you could make it easier?

ACTION Before you drive somewhere today, plan ahead of time what you'll do in the car.

75 What offends you owns you.

The greatest way to make enemies in my neighborhood is to claim chairs at the communal pool. If you come down at 10 a.m. when the pool opens and put towels over the best spot to sit and then don't return until 3 p.m., you are playing with fire. We don't have an official blackball process, but you're skating on thin ice, my friend.

One afternoon, I spent an hour staring at that exact situation. If that makes me sound petty, that's only because sometimes I am petty. But I'm also deliberate about my mindset, so I didn't hold on to the pettiness for very long. Instead, I reminded myself of this soundtrack:

What offends you owns you.

I was missing a great afternoon at the pool with my wife and kids. I felt so frustrated by what's at worst a bit of inconsiderate behavior that I might as well have not been there. I was offended to the point that this little neighborly misbehavior was owning a chunk of my day. That's pretty dumb.

My time is valuable. So is yours.

Why would we let a stranger online who has a different political belief than we do offend us?

Why would we let someone cutting us off on the way to work derail our morning?

Why would we let one rude customer at work send our entire week into a tailspin?

When you see it in black and white like that, it's obvious.

You should never let what offends you set your plans for the day. I wrote this soundtrack down in my notebook to remind myself of the truth. Then I snapped out of the bad attitude and enjoyed the rest of the day with my family.

It really can be that easy once you realize that what offends you owns you and that you don't like your big days being owned by small offenses.

QUESTION What's the last thing that really offended you? How did you get over it?

ACTION Overlook one offense today. Big, small, in-between—make a deliberate effort to let something go.

76 Am I signing the front or the back of the check?

The older I get, the more I just tend to tell people the truth.

This is not always welcomed.

When a friend recently asked me, "Can you believe my boss made me stay late on the Friday before Memorial Day?" I answered too quickly and far too honestly.

"Yes. Yes, I can believe that. She signs the front of your checks." If you're a lot younger than me, signing the front of a check means she's the one paying you.

That is not what my friend wanted to hear, but it is true. Today's is a simple soundtrack that will save you so much frustration in your career:

Am I signing the front or the back of the check?

If you are signing the front of the check, you are the client or the boss. You are the one who has the right to make the decisions, set the expectations, and run the show. If you are signing the back of the check, you are an employee. You can certainly quit the company or fire the client, but otherwise it's your job to do the work.

My friend was signing the back of the check, therefore he was expected to stay late. That's not fun, but getting paid is. Having a job is. Being able to send your kids to college is.

The flip side is that if you're signing the front of the check, you better be the one leading. You have a lot of responsibility. You steer the ship. If it hits rocks, guess who gets called into an even bigger office with an even bigger person who is signing your checks? You.

It goes both ways.

The next time you're frustrated because people are asking you so many questions and bringing you so many problems, remind yourself that's part of signing the front of the check. The next time a boss expects you to get there early or stay late, remind yourself that's part of signing the back of the check.

The work is a lot easier to do when you realize which side you're on.

QUESTION If you're not happy with which side of the check you're on, what can you do about it?

ACTION Take the answer to that question, find a coffee shop you like, and come up with three small actions you could take today.

77 Has that ever happened before?

Jim Gaffigan does not hate me. I was worried he might, but it turns out he doesn't.

We crossed paths about fifteen years ago when I asked him to endorse my book *Do Over*. Asking people to endorse your book is one of my least favorite parts of being an author. What if they say no? What if they never respond to your request? What if they go the extra mile and say, "I read your book and it's terrible. I hate you."

That's what I was worried Jim Gaffigan would do. Instead, he graciously agreed, quickly wrote an endorsement, and then wished me the best with the launch of the book.

What's your least favorite part of your job? Every job has something. Maybe you hate budget season. Maybe it's the quarterly meeting where you have to present in front of all your peers. Maybe it's managing people much older or younger than you. It could be anything, and when you think of it, your fear paints the worst-case scenario. The budget will be so bad your boss fires you on the spot. You forget your place in the speech and your pants catch on fire. The older people you manage are resentful you're the leader, and the younger people use slang that confuses you. Bet.

Here's a soundtrack for those exact moments:

Has that ever happened before?

The thing you're afraid of—has it happened before? Did you get fired the last time you presented the budget, or did you just get feedback? Did the speech go fine? Did the people you manage manage to be managed? Did Jim Gaffigan say that he hates you?

Chances are, the thing you're so worried about has never happened and probably never will. Don't let your broken soundtracks tell you any different. Don't let your broken mindset predict the worst around every corner. Don't let your broken mindset hold you back from that thing you need to do.

Has that ever happened before? Nope. And it won't happen this time either.

QUESTION | What's your silliest, most extreme fear about the thing you need to do? (In this chapter I used the example of your pants catching on fire. Get that silly with your answer.)

ACTION | Laugh at your fear and do it anyway.

78 Start a streak.

I broke a nineteen-day streak yesterday.

For nineteen days in a row, I walked at least 10,000 steps. That ended yesterday at 10:30 p.m. when I went to bed with only 6,100 steps.

In the past, one of two things would have happened:

1. I would have left the friends we are hosting in our mountain house and spent time running by myself to make sure I hit my goal.
2. I would have beat myself up today, felt discouraged, and not tracked my steps for the next month. (I used to be the Mike Tyson of beating myself up.)

In that first scenario, I would have abandoned my wife to host our friends by herself so that I could maintain a streak that I was not getting paid for, was not life-threatening, and was not benefiting anyone but me. "You guys are going to lunch? I can't join you. I work for my Garmin watch now." In that second scenario, I would have lost a month of progress to a day of imperfection. Instead, I taught myself a new soundtrack:

Start a streak.

That's all I'm going to do when I break a streak—I'll start a new one. I'll set a ten-minute timer and then write down everything I learned by breaking the last one (e.g., next time get up early before everyone else to go for a quick run). Then I will start a new streak.

Did you know you could do that—just start a new streak? You don't have to mourn the last one. You don't have to roll around in shame. You don't have to reexamine your entire life and dig deep to find the root causes of your bad behavior. Imagine me spending hundreds of dollars lying on a couch and telling a therapist, "Maybe my dad didn't hug me enough when I was a kid or teach me how to use tools. That's why my step goal failed."

Start a streak (SAS).

Throw a little SAS at your goal. Respond to your perfectionism with SAS. Give your fear a mouthful of SAS.

When you miss a day, start a streak. When you fall short, start a streak. When you drop the ball, start a streak.

You have permission to begin again.

Start a streak!

QUESTION | What's a streak you've broken that you were disappointed about?

ACTION | Start it again today.

79 Kids care about your clock, not your career.

I used to want my kids to be proud of me. It made me feel good whenever someone recognized me at Costco and told me in front of them, "I loved your book!" I felt a burst of happiness because inside I was thinking, "See, kids, your dad is doing stuff. I have a cool job!"

But do you know what I realized over the years?

Kids care about your clock, not your career.

They don't care what you do for a living. They don't care if you've got an important job in an important office. They don't care about your title, your prestige, or any of the other work pressures you put on yourself.

Want to know if I'm telling the truth? Ask a friend's kid what their mom or dad does for a living. I asked my oldest daughter's friend what her dad did. She said, "Something with technology, I think." I found out later her dad is a very successful CEO of a company. The CEO! This was a college student I was talking to. The answers you get from younger kids are even funnier.

"My mom does something with boxes."

"My dad's in money."

"I think it's insurance or banking."

Kids don't care about your career, they care about your clock. In other words, "How much time do we get to spend together?" The rainy-day board game, the fishing trip, the unexpected ice cream run after dinner—these are the key performance indicators kids are going to look for in the fourth quarter.

I hope your job with boxes works out. I really do. But don't worry about how it impacts your kids. They'd rather you make a fort with the boxes anyway.

QUESTION | What's your kids' favorite thing to do with you?

ACTION | Plan to do that this weekend.

80 Happiness is wild expectations plus hard work and generous timelines.

"Happiness is reality minus expectations." That's a popular soundtrack that's been attributed to a few people. I don't know who first said it, but they were wrong. The gist is that the best way to be happy is to not have any expectations. If you'll just accept reality without adding any expectations to it, you'll be fine.

What? That's a dour way to go through life.

Imagine if the solution to disappointment was to never be excited in the first place. Sure, you might keep yourself safe from a little heartbreak, but you'd never get to dream. You'd have a vanilla existence. You'd quietly go through life unwilling to hope for the future, because what if those hopes don't come true? Better to pre-disappoint yourself now than to have reality disappoint you later.

Borrrrrrring. Here's a much better soundtrack:

Happiness is wild expectations plus hard work and generous timelines.

Don't just have expectations—have wild expectations. Expect your kids to get into college. Expect your book to get published. Expect your retirement to be fantastic. Expect your business to be profitable. Expect your marriage to be awesome. Expect your exercise plan to be successful. Shoot for the moon in every single area of your life.

And then put in a lot of hard work and give yourself a generous amount of time to accomplish it. That last part is something most people miss. True disappointment is often a by-product of an unrealistic timeline. You wanted the weight to drop off faster. You wanted the business to make money faster. You wanted your teenagers to make it through the challenges of adolescence faster. When none of that happened fast enough, you felt crushed.

Let's make sure that never happens again to either of us. Amplify your hope. Make it big and bold and above all wild. Life is too short for safe expectations.

Put in the work. Outwork your fear. Outwork your insecurity. Outwork your competition. Outwork your bills. Then give it time. More time than you want to. More time than you expected. More time than you ever thought it would take. Never let the pace of the progress discourage you.

Happiness is wild expectations plus hard work and generous timelines.

QUESTION Of the three ingredients—expectations, hard work, and timelines—which one is most challenging for you?

ACTION If you are working on a goal right now, double each of the ingredients to see how fun things could really be.

81 I don't wallow.

I retired from breakup songs fifteen years ago.

There wasn't an official ceremony. I don't remember the exact date it happened. I couldn't tell you the last one I listened to. I just decided one day to stop listening to sad music. That might not seem like a big deal to you, but for someone who's favorite genre of music was "mopey," this was a significant decision.

What made me change?

I learned how powerful the words I put into my head are. This is going to blow your mind, but when you listen to sad music, you feel sadder. When you listen to depressing music, you feel more depressed. When you listen to dark music, you feel darker.

The reverse is true, of course. When you listen to fast music, you drive faster. When you listen to energetic music, you work out harder. That's why gyms don't play slow classical waltzes. It's also why fast-food restaurants play upbeat music during busy times. They know the music will encourage you to eat faster and leave, creating room for other customers.

This all feels so obvious now, but I promise at the time I didn't see the connection. For years I listened to Adam Duritz of Counting Crows bemoan his most recent heartbreak during my entire commute to work. Then I'd wonder why I felt down all day.

I didn't have a soundtrack to capture this decision until I overheard my oldest daughter L.E. telling a friend why she didn't like rewatching sad movies over and over again. In the kitchen I heard her say, "I don't wallow." What a word! When you listen to sad music, wear sad clothes with statements like "Adulting is hard," or drink out of a coffee cup that says "Don't grow up, it's a trap," you are wallowing in negative emotions.

I feel sad sometimes. Life is not easy and comes with its fair share of heartaches that I process openly. I'd never tell you to eliminate any emotion that's healthy, and sadness is certainly one of them. But I'd also never tell you to rehearse sadness, to use it as a form of entertainment, or to wallow in a song, movie, or personal regret.

Breakup songs are for moody teenagers. That's not us.

QUESTION Where do you tend to wallow when it comes to entertainment?

ACTION Add a little bit of positive entertainment to your life.

82 The old me doesn't exist anymore.

The worst version of me was the Atlanta version.

I don't blame the city, although the traffic definitely didn't help. Highway 400 steals a tiny bit of your soul every time you commute to work, but it really wasn't Atlanta's fault. They do have a pretty nice aquarium after all.

I just made the most knuckleheaded decisions of my life when I lived in Atlanta. I wasn't present in my marriage, I was fumbling as a father, I was a terrible employee, and I was out of shape. If there was a mistake to be made, I made it in Atlanta.

We haven't lived there in seventeen years, and the life I have now looks nothing like that one. But every now and then a broken soundtrack tells me, "You're only one misstep from returning to the worst version of yourself." Have you ever felt that way? If you haven't, thank goodness these essays are short. If you have, I hope you'll practice this soundtrack:

The old me doesn't exist anymore.

It doesn't.

That person is gone. You're not teetering on the edge of becoming that person again with every decision you make. You're not one bad mistake away from becoming exactly who you used to be. You're not one disastrous week away from becoming whatever your version of the Atlanta you is.

You have different friends now. You have different skills now. You have different beliefs now. I bet the old you wouldn't have even read a book like this.

It took me years to learn this soundtrack, but I hope it only takes you minutes now that I've written it down. The old you is gone. Enjoy the current you. I bet the people who love you would tell you the same.

? QUESTION What was the city you thought of when I said mine was Atlanta? If you've moved away, has all of you left that city yet?

ACTION Ask someone you trust if you're a different person than you were a decade ago.

83 Some beats none.

My coworker Bill Hampton hates this soundtrack. Every time I say it, he grimaces. It's frustrating to him that in twelve years of writing about soundtracks this has become one of the ones most repeated by readers.

Why doesn't he like it?

Because he's not a perfectionist.

If he was, he'd see the immediate appeal in it.

As I said earlier, perfectionists only have two speeds: all or nothing. Either they do a goal completely or they don't even try. That doesn't sound like a problem until you realize that most perfectionists never even try. I know perfectionists who have been waiting for ten years to write their book. They don't want to start it until they are sure it will be amazing. I know perfectionists who want to walk ten thousand steps every day. If they can't one day because they're busy, they won't accept just walking six thousand. They decide to not even try. It's all or nothing, so they choose nothing.

That's when I tell them this soundtrack:

Some beats none.

If you want to write one thousand words a day but have time for only five hundred, some beats none.

If you want to call ten potential clients but can only contact four, some beats none.

If you want to clean your entire kitchen but can only do the dishes, some beats none.

If you're a perfectionist, you often feel the pressure to choose between all or none. Life rarely offers us the time or opportunity to do all, especially with our busy schedules, but some is always available.

And some, my fellow perfectionists, beats none.

QUESTION What part of your life is too perfectionistic right now? What would doing "some" look like?

ACTION Today, when you catch yourself saying, "I'm too busy to do _______," do some of that activity.

84 Bigger than bored, smaller than stressed.

I don't know all the secrets to life, but I do know this one.

If you want to have a happy, fulfilling life, the kind you dreamed of when you were a little kid and your third-grade teacher asked what you wanted to be when you grew up, all you have to do is live out this soundtrack:

Bigger than bored, smaller than stressed.

Find work, hobbies, and relationships that aren't boring. If your job is mindless, if your hobbies are too easy, if your relationships are too dull, you will be underchallenged. You will rust from lack of effort. On the flip side, if your job is overwhelming, if your hobbies are impossible, if your relationships are chaotic, you will be overchallenged. You will burn out from too much effort.

How do you know when you've found this mythical sweet spot? You try.

You never know before you do the thing if the thing is going to deliver just the right amount of challenge. You can't possibly guess that beforehand. It's a mystery you can only solve through action. But with a little bit of self-awareness, you can learn to easily spot when you've found your Goldilocks moment with any given activity. With a little testing, you'll know that it's just right—not too hot, not too cold, not too big, not too small.

I know I'm not in my zone when I have a perfectly manicured inbox. I must be bored at work or home if I've got the energy to sculpt my Gmail like Michelangelo. Whenever I catch myself doing that, I ask, "I wonder what challenging project I'm avoiding right now?" On the other end of the spectrum, I know I've flown too close to the sun and surpassed my capacity based on how short I am with people. I am at my grumpiest when I have bit off more than I can chew and probably need to pull back a bit.

I can't tell you where your exact spot is, just that it will expand as your capacity does. The black belt in karate doesn't find the white belt exercises engaging any longer.

What I can tell you is that most people don't push themselves out of their comfort zone and have a hard time escaping the boring end of the spectrum. We are the worst judge of what we are capable of, and if there's one mistake people make, it's playing it too safe. I do meet people who are shooting too high with expectations, but they are rare. Most people apply the brakes too quickly versus sitting on the gas pedal too long.

Why have I written twelve nonfiction books? Because writing just one would have been boring. Why haven't I written twelve fiction books? Because that genre is beyond the limits of my abilities. For now.

QUESTION On a scale from 1 (plays it safe) to 10 (lives on the edge), where would you rate yourself?

ACTION Find the most boring part of your life and add one exciting action to it today. For example, volunteer for a new project at work.

85 Wisdom adds. Worry subtracts.

Do you know what the most distracting thing in the world is?

It's not Instagram.

It's not TikTok.

It's not Facebook.

It's not your phone or your TV.

It's worry.

Nothing costs you more time, more energy, more creativity, more productivity, and ultimately more life than worry. I should know. Until I started using soundtracks in my mid-thirties, I was a professional worrier.

I spent at least three hours each day, every day, overthinking every single facet of my existence. Before I drove to work, I'd worry about how bad the traffic would be. On the way to work, I'd worry about work. At work, I'd worry about who I'd go to lunch with. After lunch, I'd worry about how bad the traffic would be on the way home. On the way home, I'd worry about my marriage. At night I'd worry about work the next day. Now that I think about it, three hours a day might be a low estimate for how much I worried.

Do you know how good I'd be at jujitsu if I practiced three hours a day for thirty years? Do you know how rich I'd be if I did a side hustle for three hours a day for thirty years? Do you know how many friends I'd have if I spent three hours a day for thirty years working on my relationships?

Worry subtracts. It always steals resources from you. On the flip side, wisdom adds. When I spend thirty minutes running in my neighborhood, I have added twelve hours of feeling great. That's a wise decision. When I spend sixty minutes writing thank-you notes, I am adding years of great relationships to my life. That's a wise decision. When I spend months paying off debt, I am adding decades of financial freedom to my life. That's a wise decision.

I could worry about all of those things instead—my health, my friends, my finances—but that wouldn't add anything. That would only subtract the time, and at this point I'm a bit addicted to addition.

Wisdom adds. Worry subtracts. Choose wisely.

QUESTION | What's one wise decision you could choose today that's a good use of your time?

ACTION | Go do it.

86 Doubts are a dare.

I hope everyone you know believes in every dream you have.

I hope no one online ever says a discouraging comment about your goal.

I hope friends, family, neighbors, and strangers in the street shower you with unwavering support.

But in the very likely case that you live in the real world, not the fantasy one I just described, I hope you will hold on to this soundtrack:

Doubts are a dare.

I used to get sad when people doubted I could accomplish something. I wanted the whole world to root for me. Someone's doubt would turn into discouragement, which would turn into delay. A single negative comment could throw me for a loop for a few hours or even a few days. But then I decided to believe this soundtrack. I started seeing doubts as dares.

What if you did that too?

What if every boss who doubted you was really daring you to get a better job?

What if every online commenter who doubted you was daring you to get better at your craft?

What if every friend who doubted you could grow your business was daring you to not give up?

Challenge accepted. Now the doubts don't delay me from the work, they drive me to it. Now I don't fear them coming, I just flip them into a tiny spark of motivation.

Can you imagine how much easier your life would be if you saw doubts that way?

I dare you to try.

QUESTION When was a time someone doubted your abilities? What were they daring you to do?

ACTION Think of a friend who might be struggling with doubt. Send them an encouraging text.

87 Accept uncertainty. Increase certainty.

Sometimes I see photos of myself from speaking events and wonder, “Who is that white-haired man onstage?”

It’s me. About three years ago my head shifted from “lightly gray” to “I bet he likes World War II documentaries.” There’s no going back. If I tried to dye it now, I’d look like your grandfather trying to casually say “rizz” in conversations.

All those extra years have come with a little bit of extra wisdom though. One thing you learn as you get older is that a lot of life comes down to your ability to hold two opposite ideas in your hands at the same time. My favorite example of this principle involves certainty.

Remarkable people do two very different things all week:

1. Accept the uncertainty of life
2. Increase certainty through action

For that first point, they know so much of life is out of their control. They can't control the economy, the weather, flight delays, or other people's actions. They go with the flow when that's what's called for and don't demand certainty from the uncertain parts of life.

For the second point, they know so much of life is in their control. They are in charge of their soundtracks, their words, and their actions. They might not control whether a client buys their product, but they know if they want to increase certainty, then making a hundred sales calls sure beats making only ten.

Is life uncertain? Yes.

Can you make life more certain? Surprisingly, yes.

Accept uncertainty. Increase certainty.

QUESTION | Have you ever gotten stuck because you were waiting for something to be "certain" before you started?

ACTION | Choose one activity you've put off and schedule the first step on your calendar in the next two weeks.

88 How could this be good?

I am a negative person by nature. This surprises people sometimes given my cheery disposition on stage, in books, and online, but I assure you it is true. My default is pessimistic. My clouds are set to stormy. But years ago I learned that positivity has a much better return on investment than negativity, so I practice it enthusiastically every day.

Soundtracks like "Everything is always working out for me" help, but what do I do when something clearly disappointing has happened? I can't lie to myself and "turn a frown upside down" as if I enjoy failure. Our brains are too smart to be flat out lied to. Instead, I engage in curiosity and ask myself a simple soundtrack:

How could this be good?

It might only be a sliver, that proverbial silver lining, but with a little bit of effort, I can find the good in most situations. I started doing this when miscommunication with a client caused me some frustration. They swore they verbally changed our contract in a Zoom meeting, and I swore we never discussed that particular detail. It was the kind of situation that in the past would have cost me nights of lost sleep and possibly the entire relationship if I sat in the negativity. Instead I asked, "How could this be good?" Several days later, after I had processed the whole thing, I wrote down a list of possible ways. Here are a few:

1. This is an invitation to introspection. I overreacted in this moment. I wonder what that means? What a great chance to develop some deeper self-awareness.
2. If I had an AI notetaker turned on in Zoom, I would have a record I could check. This is a good reason to start doing that, and in the future it might save me even more frustration if this kind of thing happens again.

3. I get to practice my leadership with my team. They're all frustrated too, so I get to be the one with the cool head.
4. I can write about this.

I ended up listing ten different reasons this might be good, and all of them were a lot more honest and practical than "turn a frown upside down."

Being positive doesn't mean you won't go through negative situations. It means that when you do, you turn your thoughts into actions and your actions into results. I wanted a stronger relationship with this client, so I retired my broken soundtracks and came up with a simple action—a list—that would help me get there.

The next time you go through a difficult situation, don't sit in it any longer than you need to. When you're ready, grab a piece of paper. Write "How could this be good?" at the top and go.

QUESTION | What's one hardship you're currently going through or have recently gone through?

ACTION | Find the silver lining!

89 Stop. Start. Better.

This soundtrack is worth $6,000.

We should have put that on the cover of the book. "You'll find $6,000 on page 240!" But then you would have flipped all the way to the end of the book while browsing in the airport store and felt tricked. "Aw man, there's not money tucked into this book. Just wisdom!" Then I would have said, "Wisdom is worth more than rubies." You would have replied, "Who measures value in rubies anymore? What are you, a thousand years old?" That's not at all how I want this relationship to go.

So, where is the $6,000? Well, it's more of a savings really, because that's how much money I've spent on personal development books over the last thirty years but you won't have to. I've read four hundred books at an average cost of $15 each, in case you're curious about the math. But you can skip them and buy a Jet Ski instead.

There are only three ways to improve your life:

1. Stop doing something.
2. Start doing something.
3. Get better at something you're already doing.

Stop doubting. Stop undercharging for your work. Stop buying that food you can't really keep in the house without eating the entire container in one sitting. Stop hanging out with that friend who encourages your worst decisions. Stop waiting for a dating relationship to magically get better and decide to end it.

Start believing. Start repeating new soundtracks. Start asking for more projects at work so it's easier to get recognized and rewarded at the end of the year. Start writing down three things a day you are grateful for. Start exercising three times a week. Start posting on LinkedIn more consistently. Start a new hobby to relax on the weekends.

Get better at asking questions. Get better at cycling so you can complete that century ride that's always been on your list. Get serious about your garden because it flips all your switches. Get better at walking your dog, because an overweight pet means an underattentive owner. (They can't buy their own food—somebody is doing this to them and it's not Rover.) Get better at writing that book you've been dragging around for years.

Stop. Start. Better. Three words that sum up thirty years of personal development.

QUESTION | Which of those three actions jumped out at you? What's one thing you could do to move in that direction today?

ACTION | Do it.

90 Negotiations are over.

At 7 a.m. on a Monday I made a plan for my month. (A guy who writes a book titled *Procrastination Proof* better have a lot of plans to get into motion!)

By 8 a.m. my broken soundtracks were already trying to talk me out of the plan. "Do we really need to run that many times this week? Are you sure we have to eat less queso at night when we're watching TV? Is it necessary to get up so early every morning?"

The chatter got louder and louder as I continued my day, until I said one of my favorite soundtracks:

"Negotiations are over."

The plan wasn't up for debate. The decisions had been made. The commitment was done. I don't know why my broken soundtracks thought they could call me back to the table, but they can't. Negotiations are over.

How do you end them? Well, that's up to you. Maybe once you've made a firm decision you need to print it out and sign it. Throw a date on the document, too, so that if your broken soundtracks get mouthy you can say, "On October 14 we swore we'd do this." Maybe you should tell a friend. Whenever I have big goals, I text my buddy Bill Buntyn. I don't mean once. I mean that if I have a forty-day goal, I text him every morning for forty days in a row. I need daily accountability sometimes. Maybe you need a chart or a checklist to formalize that negotiations are over.

Get creative! New habits, new behavior, new goals can be hard to establish. Don't be afraid to use as many tools as you need to make the new soundtrack stick.

My broken soundtracks didn't want to write this entry. It was way too pretty outside. Instagram was far too interesting. I could have pushed the project off until tomorrow, next week, or even next month. But I didn't.

Negotiations were over.

QUESTION Do you ever second-guess yourself after you've made a decision?

ACTION Commit to one small decision today and hold on to that commitment. When you've accomplished it, make a note of how you felt, or text your own Bill Buntyn and let him know you did it.

CONCLUSION

A friend recently asked me a question about movies that caught me off guard. He said, "What's your favorite movie and who is the character you identify with?"

I instantly knew the answer to the first part of that question: *Good Will Hunting.*

That's my favorite movie. I grew up in Massachusetts and first saw it when I was in college in Birmingham, Alabama. I was homesick for the Northeast, and everything from the accents to the attitudes felt like the neighborhood I desperately missed.

My answer to the second part of the question surprised me though.

In my early twenties, I most related to Will Hunting, played by Matt Damon. If you haven't seen the movie, he was a math prodigy working as a janitor. Through a series of events his immense talent is discovered, and he embarks on a new life guided by a wise guru of a counselor played by Robin Williams. When I watched it, I wanted to feel special too. I felt stuck and frustrated, hoping that maybe I had a special talent the world had never seen. I wanted to be discovered and, if possible, even say Matt Damon's signature line: "How do you like them apples?"

I felt that way for years, but this time, when I answered my friend's question, I found myself saying, "I identify with Robin Williams's character." Now in my fifties, I'm not waiting to be discovered. I realized in my mid-thirties that how I think about me is up to me. With a little bit of work, I could build the kind of mindset that propels me forward instead of holding me back.

I was the cavalry I was waiting for. Better yet, if I was brave, I could help other people make the same discovery. I could be the one telling the Matt Damons they are capable of so much more than they think.

That was always my goal with this little book.

I think you're built for adventures.

I think you're meant for great relationships.

I think you're destined for engaging careers, financial freedom, and health goals that last a lot longer than New Year's resolutions.

I think when your thoughts turn into actions, your actions will turn into results and you can accomplish more than you ever imagined.

Above all, regardless of your age, I think you're just getting started.

What's next?

I don't have a Capital One in my wallet, but I do have something even better. I have a soundtrack.

It's true, at any given moment I have a few soundtracks with me. They're posted by my computer too. They're in notes inside my phone. They're scribbled down in every notebook I use. Why? Because mindset isn't an event, it's a practice. The best things in life always are. Imagine if I told you the key to having a great marriage is to talk to your spouse for two hours once a month. That's all you have to do, have one meaningful conversation once a month and you'll be golden.

No, if you want a great marriage, you work on it daily.

If you want to be in shape, you work on it daily.

If you want to be rich, you work on it daily.

If you want a winning mindset, guess how often you work on it? Daily.

It's not complicated. In fact, I boiled the whole process down to what I call "the 3 R's."

I wrote about them extensively in my book *Soundtracks*. You should read that one next. It's your go-to, how-to guide to building a winning mindset. The summary is simple. If you want to build a fantastic mindset, all you have to do is:

Retire your broken soundtracks. The next time you find yourself playing a negative, unhelpful soundtrack, see how fast you can catch it. Hit pause as it speeds by and ask yourself, "Do I want to keep listening to that?"

Replace them with new soundtracks. If the answer is no, find a new soundtrack to listen to instead. There are ninety to choose from in this book, I share new ones on all my social media channels @JonAcuff, and you're probably already noticing them in your day-to-day life.

Repeat the new ones so often they become as automatic as the old ones. Should you write that great soundtrack on a Post-it? Should you share it with a friend? Should you make it your phone lock-screen? Should you get a T-shirt with it? Yes. This is no time to worry about being too cheesy. Your mindset is worth pursuing with consistency, creativity, and enthusiasm. Repeat! Repeat! Repeat!

If you do those three things regularly, you'll look up one day soon and be surprised at how many new thoughts, new actions, and new results you've got in your life.

Most people won't believe it's that easy.

Most people won't believe it's that fast.

Most people won't believe something that simple changed you that much. But you know what we say?

How do you like them apples?

No, that's not it. Wrong line, Matt Damon. What do we say?

We're not most people!

—Jon

ACKNOWLEDGMENTS

Even small books take big teams!

To Jenny, L.E., and McRae—long before these soundtracks were in a book, we said them in our house. I'm so grateful I get to be on your team!

Ashley Holland, this is book number seven we've done together! If you ever retire, that will be the day I do too. We're just getting started! Caleb Peavy, thanks for believing in the idea of soundtracks long before anyone else did. Gian Lemmi, my favorite thing about you is that no matter the challenge we throw at you, your answer is always the same: "I can figure that out!" Brandi Spurling, you helped me turn a list of hundreds of soundtracks into ninety tight, insightful entries. Thanks for kicking each one of these pages back and forth with me.

Massive thank you to everyone at Baker Publishing. Whenever another author tells me they're having a hard time with their publishing team, I keep my mouth shut because working with you guys is a breeze. Brian Vos, from subtle edits to massive ideas, you never fail to make every book I write even better! Eileen Hanson, thanks for the acorn! It was a great visual for how many ideas you have for marketing that always turn into expansive forests! Amy Nemecek, I don't know how you do it, but book after book, you overdeliver with laser-pointed feedback.

William Overbeeke and Dan Pitts, thanks for making sure the design always matches the strength of the words. Kelli Smith, thanks for faithfully spearheading the publicity side of things. Nathan Henrion, Bob Gaudet, and the entire sales and marketing teams, thanks for getting this book in hands and homes. Alex Nieuwsma and Naomi Zylstra, these books go worldwide because of your hard work. Thank you! Mike Salisbury and Curtis Yates, great books need great literary agents. Thanks for more than a decade of being mine!

NOTES

1. Joseph Epstein, "Think You Have a Book in You? Think Again," *The New York Times*, September 28, 2002, https://www.nytimes.com/2002/09/28/opinion/think-you-have-a-book-in-you-think-again.html.

2. Jodie Cook, "Why 92% of People Fail to Achieve Their Goals and What to Do Instead," *Forbes*, June 27, 2025, https://www.forbes.com/sites/jodiecook/2025/06/27/why-92-of-people-fail-to-achieve-their-goals-and-what-to-do-instead/.

3. "Amid the Fragmented TV Landscape, Time Spent with Content Is the Best Planning Data There Is," Nielsen, January 2024, https://www.nielsen.com/insights/2024/amid-the-fragmented-tv-landscape-time-spent-with-content-is-the-best-planning-data-there-is/.

4. Paul Krugman, "Why Most Economists' Predictions Are Wrong," *Red Herring*, June 1998, 28, https://issuu.com/jasonpontin/docs/red_herring-june_1998.

5. Steven Pressfield, *The War of Art* (Black Irish Entertainment LLC, 2002), 166.

JON ACUFF is the *New York Times* bestselling author of twelve books, including *Procrastination Proof*, *Soundtracks: The Surprising Solution to Overthinking*, and the *Wall Street Journal* #1 bestseller *Finish: Give Yourself the Gift of Done*. His books have sold more than a million copies in dozens of languages around the world. When he's not writing or recording his popular podcast, *All It Takes Is a Goal*, Acuff can be found on a stage as one of INC's Top 100 Leadership Speakers. He's spoken to hundreds of thousands of people at conferences, colleges, and companies, including FedEx, Range Rover, Microsoft, and Comedy Central. Known for his insights wrapped in humor, Acuff's fresh perspective on life has given him the opportunity to write for *Fast Company*, *Harvard Business Review*, and *Time* magazine. Jon lives outside of Nashville, Tennessee, with his wife, Jenny, and two daughters, the authors L.E. and McRae. To learn more, visit JonAcuff.com.

CONNECT WITH JON

JonAcuff.com
@AuthorJonAcuff
@JonAcuff
@JonAcuff